Close Encounters
Dance Partners for Creativity

Close Encounters
Dance Partners for Creativity

*Kerry Chappell, Linda Rolfe,
Anna Craft and Veronica Jobbins*

Trentham Books

Stoke on Trent, UK and Sterling, USA

Trentham Books Limited
Westview House   22883 Quicksilver Drive
734 London Road   Sterling
Oakhill   VA 20166-2012
Stoke on Trent   USA
Staffordshire
England ST4 5NP

First published 2011

British Library Cataloguing-in-Publication Data
A catalogue record for this book is available from the British Library

Credit: Figure 1 in chapter 4 provided by Tony Nandi.

All other photographs taken by the authors.

Cover photography by Kerry Chappell.

ISBN 978-1-85856-487-6

Designed and typeset by Trentham Books Ltd, Chester
Printed and bound in Great Britain by 4edge Ltd, Hockley

Contents

Acknowledgments

The DPC university team express their thanks to the Arts and Humanities Research Council for the research grant (Grant number: AH/F010168/1) which made the project behind this book possible. We are also grateful for in-kind support from Trinity Laban.

In addition there are many individuals who have contributed in various capacities to whom we are very grateful. This includes all our co-researchers in each of the research sites and the schools, organisations and dance companies of which they are a part; Debbie Watson for manuscript reading and insightful and sensitive additional analysis which contributes to underpinning Chapters 9 and 10; Margo Greenwood for professional photography, work on the website, the practitioner resource and seminar assistance; Maria Gregoriou for persisting with site access documentation; David McCormick and Sky Neal for filming and editing; Chu-Yun for seminar assistance; Linda McConnell for speedy transcription; Scott Walker for translating scribbles into intelligible digitised visuals; and Jane Woolley for very informative feedback on the manuscript.

We also thank key University of Exeter staff, including Research Support from Tamara Snell and Karan Ogden; and Technical Support from Mike Jeffries and Richard Osborne.

We are grateful to Gillian Klein for recognising the potential in our book proposal, and for her ongoing guidance – and to the team at Trentham for their support in the production of what we hope will be a useful text for a wide audience.

Finally, we thank our families and close friends and colleagues for their encouragement, patience and faith.

Kerry Chappell, Linda Rolfe, Anna Craft, Veronica Jobbins
April, 2011

The contributors

Helen Angove graduated from Royal Holloway, University of London in 1990 with a BA (Hons) in Drama and Theatre after which she completed a Postgraduate Diploma (Dist) in Community Dance at Laban. She holds an MA (Dist) in Dance Studies and will complete her PhD in 2012. Having begun her career as a secondary school dance teacher in 1992, she worked in Further and Higher Education in various roles, retaining a focus on pedagogy and quality assurance. She spent an inspiring year in 2008 as a community dance artist in Somerset, and then became Course Leader for the new University Campus Suffolk BA (Hons) Dance in the Community. As a member of a Dance Training and Accreditation Partnership Professional Standards Working Group, Helen has contributed to the development of National Occupational Standards in Dance Leadership. She also sits on the Regional Dance Advisory Group for Youth Dance England.

Kerry Chappell (PhD) is a part-time Research Fellow in the Exeter University Graduate School of Education. Her research investigates how we conceive of and work for creativity (within dance education and generically), and developing this meaningfully within educational futures. Most recently this has centred on DPC, as well as working with Anna Craft on the Aspire Programme (www.education.exeter.ac.uk/aspire), which facilitates student-led school change. Kerry also carries out consultancy which includes working as the creativity researcher with Trinity Laban dance scientists on the Leverhulme-funded dance Centres for Advanced Training research (www.trinitylaban.ac.uk/dance-science). Methodologically, Kerry researches co-participatively with adults and students, as well as using mixed methods with quantitatively-oriented research colleagues. Future foci include investigating interdisciplinary collaborative creativity with science and arts colleagues. Kerry's research is informed by her practice as a dance artist and previous aikido practice (Ni-Dan), as well as her time as a dance education manager at Laban (1998-2003).

Anna Craft is Professor of Education at the University of Exeter and The Open University. She works with learners, teachers, researchers and policymakers in England and abroad to develop imagination, creativity and educational futures. A qualitative researcher, committed research leader and teacher, Anna leads studies on Possibility Thinking and learner voice, as well as creative partnership. At Exeter she teaches Masters and doctoral students in the areas of creativity, the arts and educational futures. She leads the CREATE research group (http://www.education.ex.uk/create). At the Open University she works on the foundation degree programme, the Master's programme, supervises doctoral students and co-leads a research grouping around creative teaching and learning.

She is co-Founding Editor of the peer review journal *Thinking Skills and Creativity* and co-convenes the British Educational Research Association Special Interest Group, *Creativity in Education*. She publishes extensively in the area of creativity and educational futures.

Sian Goss has worked at Brockhill Park Performing Arts College within a successful department of six dance specialists for nine years. Her experience is wide ranging, covering vocational and traditional curriculum courses. In addition, partnerships with National School of Creativity, Find Your Talent, Youth Dance England and Youth Dance have afforded her opportunities to work not only with school but the wider community. Sian has developed an interest in the impact Dance can have on effective learning across the curriculum and her work is supporting the school in driving up standards.

Rachelle Green has worked as a community dance practitioner for 15 years. She graduated from Laban with a Post Graduate Diploma in Community Dance and has since managed and delivered work across the community. She co-ordinated and delivered on the Greenwich Dance Agency community dance programme (1999-2004). And she was Deputy Director of Dance at Take Art in Somerset, where she managed and delivered a range of dance and health projects (2004-2009). In 2009 she returned to freelance practice, performing and teaching for early years, people with learning disabilities and older people. She also continued to mentor dance artists and report on Take Art's dance and health projects, as well as speaking at 5 dance and health conferences. Rachelle has recently established the company Core Dance, partly born out of the DPC research and dialogues. The company is currently delivering an integrated performance project for adults with learning disabilities.

Veronica Jobbins (MA, FRSA) is Head of Professional and Community Studies at Trinity Laban where she directs the Education and Community Programme and lectures in Dance Education. She originally trained as a specialist dance teacher before teaching for 20 years in London secondary schools and further education colleges, including time as an advisory teacher with the Inner London Education Authority PE Inspectorate. Veronica has taken an active interest in promoting and developing dance in schools throughout her career and was instrumental in the formation of the UK National Dance Teachers' Association in 1988, of which she was Chairperson until 2008. She regularly writes for dance and arts journals and presents at conferences in the UK and abroad. She also serves on a number of dance, arts and education panels and working groups concerned with dance artist training, youth dance and dance in the curriculum.

Bim Malcomson works as a choreographer, teacher and mentor. In the role of Artist in Education for the Dance Partnership and Access Department, at the Royal Ballet School, she leads creative workshops, choreographs large-scale works, bringing together Royal Ballet and state school students and is a mentor for Youth Dance England's, *Young Creatives.* As a teacher Bim works for the Centre for Advanced Training at Trinity Laban where she teaches ballet and choreography. She has also taught ballet at Lewisham College and for the Centre for Advanced Training at The Place. Bim has her own youth ballet class at Urdang Academy. Currently she is bringing together young people from different dance styles and backgrounds to create a work to be performed at The Royal Opera House.

Abi Mortimer has a first class degree at BA and MA level in dance from the University of Chichester and was awarded the Hayes Award for her contribution to the arts. She Co-founded Lîla Dance in 2005 and the company became a creative associate of The Point, Eastleigh in 2006, receiving mentorship from Hofesh Shechter and obtaining Arts Council funding. In her choreographic work with Lîla Dance, Abi has established collaborations with artists including: Yael Flexer, Simona Bertozzi, Jon Maya, puppetry company Blind Summit and international sound artist Robert Jarvis. Abi is an associate lecturer at the University of Chichester and is the choreographer for the current AQA GCSE set study.

Jackie Mortimer has worked in education for 36 years and has been responsible for developing dance as a discrete subject in her current school, Brockhill Park Performing Arts College (BPPAC). She is artistic director of a youth dance company – Instep – which caters for young people from over 20 schools in the region across both the primary and secondary sectors. Jackie has been a moderator, principal and chief examiner for General Certificate of Secondary Education Dance. Her most recent work involves action research focused on mixed age and gender dance companies whose aim is to produce stimulating and excellent dance and also to support the debate around excellence in learning in mixed age settings. This research has informed BPPAC's work as a National School of Creativity.

Michael Platt trained as an actor, teacher and Laban movement specialist. After a career in teaching he became a Learning and Teaching Adviser for Suffolk's Inclusive School Improvement Service, providing creative learning opportunities for young people in and through the arts, training for teachers and the development of resources to support the curriculum. Michael also works in education and community settings nationally and internationally as a teacher and choreographer. This includes work for DanceEast, the UK National Dance Agency for the Eastern Region; the National Dance Teacher's Association; The Royal Opera House; Trinity Laban; University Campus Suffolk's BA Dance in the Community; and the Laban Guild. He is the director of Suffolk Youth Theatre, one of the regions most innovative youth groups, with whom he has developed a unique performance style fusing drama, dance, music and design.

Linda Rolfe trained as a dance teacher, working in schools and as an advisory teacher. She has also directed youth dance companies for many years. Currently a senior lecturer at the Graduate School of Education, University of Exeter, she leads the Secondary PGCE Dance and Masters in Creative Arts courses. Linda has been an OFSTED inspector for dance and is currently a lead assessor for the Council for Dance Education and Training. Her publications include books and articles on dance education and she is the editor of the international journal Research in Dance Education.

Caroline Watkins studied dance at The London Contemporary Dance School and Laban. Currently Caroline leads a department of dance teachers at Dagenham Park Church of England School which achieved Arts College status ten years ago. Throughout her teaching career she has developed opportunities to exemplify best practice including training PGCE teachers at The Royal Academy of Dance and through professional projects and case studies for National Dance Teachers' Association and Arts Council England: Creative Partnerships. Caroline has forged several high profile partnerships with national and international dance organisations including The Royal Ballet School and Laban. She is currently developing cross Atlantic collaborations with schools in Phoenix Arizona and Los Angeles.

Helen Wright has a BA Hons in Creative Arts from Manchester Metropolitan University (1991-1994) and a PGSE in Drama from the University of Central England (1995-1996). From there she was appointed Teacher in Charge of Drama at The Grays School, Essex where she worked for 2 years before returning home to Ipswich where she worked for 11 years in local schools including Northgate High School as Head of Drama and Holywells High School as Joint Acting Head of Expressive Arts. She has always been involved in the Arts, particularly Drama and Music and spent many years supporting the County Council's Music Service assisting with the Suffolk Youth Orchestra's annual residential courses. She has travelled extensively throughout South East Asia, Australia and South and Central America and is currently working in Ipswich as a Family Intervention Project Officer, supporting at risk families to implement lasting change.

Foreword

Christopher Bannerman

This is an important book for all who are concerned about education, and it appears at a critical juncture. While its starting point and main concerns cohere around dance in schools, the implications are far-reaching and raise key questions for the future of education as a whole. This is timely and more widely relevant as profound changes are facing virtually every aspect of public life in the UK – changes which may be destined to reverberate throughout much of the western world. The authors do not merely offer an intellectually penetrating critique of these developments; rather they embrace the role of research as emancipation and offer strategies for change as part of a 'quiet revolution' (Chapter 11).

These wider perspectives are grounded in specific research initiatives in the form of collaborative projects involving dance artists and school teachers as partner researchers alongside university researchers. Dance Partners for Creativity worked in schools with young people aged 11 to 14, engaging them in creative learning processes. So the considerations of policy arise from particular experiences of practice, and this progression is achieved seamlessly and is articulated with an exemplary clarity of language that is designed to communicate to, and engage with, a wide audience. The authors have adhered to Einstein's dictum that 'everything should be as simple as it can be, but not simpler', through clear, precise prose and by avoiding simplistic reductionism through acknowledging complexity, contradiction and tension.

This is, to use a word that arises in the accounts of the practical projects, a 'brave' stance and the authors also acknowledge, with intellectual honesty, the impetus of their work: to rebalance educational policies and the practices they impose, and to achieve new visions for alternative futures for education. A key issue is the agenda of performativity, used here to denote the policy of measuring achievement in and of schools, rather than Austin's (1962) concept of performative utterances that has informed performance studies. This is identified as a key hindrance to embedding the creative learning experience in schools and the book presents practical examples and suggestions for mitigating the constraints of this agenda, and presents a conceptual map for navigating through and beyond them.

Throughout there is a strong emphasis on partnerships (between teachers, artists, university staff and students) and the book exemplifies what is being proposed: the creation of a dialogic space resulting in rich exchanges from a range of perspectives. But all are grounded in practice and a common endeavour, ensuring that a clear sense of purpose is evident throughout. The voices of partner researchers, university researchers and students offer particular perspectives and even express difference, but their common interest in experiencing meaningful, creative exchange and learning is palpable.

Dance as an embodied, social, creative activity requiring individual and group responsibility is presented as a vehicle for activating the humanising creativity that is seen as a key concern of education. The inclusive ethos of the research is mirrored by the flattened hierarchies that were observed and this is particularly significant today when there is a need for the teacher to act as a constant monitor of achievement, recording measurable outcomes from virtually every session. The partner researchers in one of the initiatives also note the activation of their own intuitive, expert-practitioner wisdom as a key aspect of the process; and observe that this often enables flexibility in both the approach and in the roles taken by each party in the partnership.

The voices of those steeped in the wisdom of practice that draws on a range of ways of knowing, including the reflective and intuitive, are clear and compelling. For example, in Chapter 3 the 'artist' and 'teacher' used their wealth of experience and knowledge to adopt more flexible professional personas and became co-explorers with the group. The result was that learning was ignited and the children 'became more demanding of each other ... more confident leaders and creators'. And in Chapter 6 we are reminded of the importance of serious play in creative learning and that the role of the teacher, within the constraints of time-tabling and targets, reports and measurement, remains: 'to ask questions, inspire and stimulate interest and to develop enquiry and interest in the world'. All the partner researchers' chapters offer unique perspectives: voices grounded in deep and broad practice, conveying the reflections of those with direct and authentic experience. They testify to the potency of the exchange between artists and teachers, between the arts and education.

The focus on exchange and partnership leads to proposals for achieving bottom-up, incremental change, the quiet revolution, which is realised through small but potent change as a means to arrive at a place where 'small-scale advocacy connects with big picture educational change' (Chapter 11). These strategies could have far reaching relevance as we face unprecedented challenges to creativity in education in the UK. For example, reductions in university funding for the Humanities have been echoed by the Arts Council England deciding in March 2011 to withdraw funding from the Creative Partnerships scheme and from Youth Dance England, both key initiatives for supporting and developing the creative potential of young people and schools. In fact a very real possibility – a possible future – is the arrival of a 'perfect storm' of quantitative agendas driven both by a desire for accountability and by short-term economic measures designed to address budget deficits, which will significantly diminish opportunities for 'creative humanism' and potentially, perhaps inadvertently, alter the UK forever.

The wider paradox is also acknowledged implicitly by the authors: sustained and sustainable economic growth can arguably be best achieved by education which instils individual and communal creativity as a preparation for an economy dependent on flexibility, individual initiative and teamwork. This seems especially pertinent to me as I am writing this in Beijing where I am co-developing a collaborative project focused on creative process with the Beijing Dance Academy and the Taipei National University of the Arts. We are navigating and negotiating our way through thickets of economic, political and social impediments as we see a way to communicate better by working together to achieve a partnership that is founded on cultural values.

Interestingly, the English language *China Daily* recently featured an article citing Lu Jun, a senior consultant at an agency affiliated to the Chinese Ministry of Education, who noted that more Chinese students are choosing to study overseas because: 'overseas schools provide a more flexible learning environment and pay more attention to ... skills such as decision-making, initiative, leadership, teamwork and sociability which are often lacking in a Chinese school's curriculum' (Ning, 2011).

These are precisely the qualities and the associated values that we are in danger of discarding, perhaps not through conscious decisions but through changes that have not been fully considered. Thus the significance of the call in this book for a wide engagement to 'support individuals interacting in partnership within culturally-grounded communities' should not be underestimated. The vision presented in this book is compelling – and it is made more so by the focus on positive practice and strategies for positive change.

Professor Christopher Bannerman
ResCen Research Centre
Middlesex University
May 2011

References

Austin, J L (1962) *How to Do Things with Words*. Oxford: Clarendon Press

Ning, Y (2011) More students choose to study abroad. *China Daily* Monday 25 April p:15 Also online at: http://www.chinadaily.com.cn/cndy/2011-04/25/content_12383944.htm

PART ONE
OPENING THE SPACE

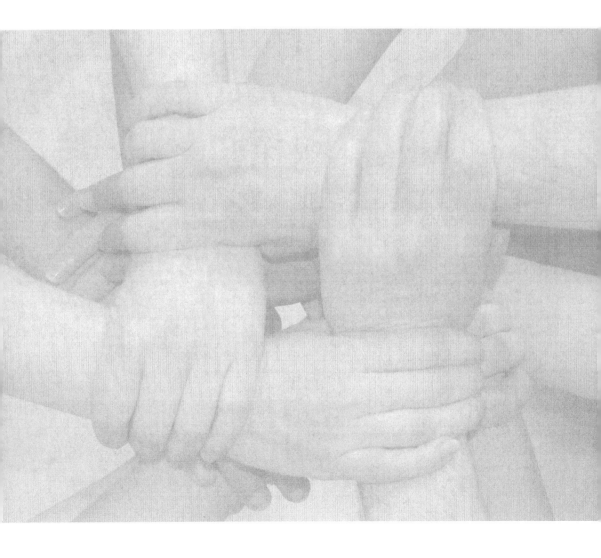

1

Introducing the research project

*Kerry Chappell, Linda Rolfe, Anna Craft
and Veronica Jobbins*

This book presents stories from the Dance Partners for Creativity (DPC) Research Project funded by the Arts and Humanities Research Council[1] from 2008 until 2010. DPC was designed to encourage enquiry, reflection and research about creativity in dance education partnership practice, and to influence practice and thinking. As the image opposite suggests, the research draws in many different people. The book features the voices of practitioner researchers, university researchers and, in parts, students, shining a spotlight on the detail of their close encounters.

Each author's story makes connections with ideas relevant to their different perspectives. Some accentuate developing practice, others reach out and build on theory, whilst others connect to education policy. As a reader, you may dip into a particular part to suit your interests. You may want to pick up on an overarching theme dealt with by different authors in relation to practice, theory and policy. However you engage with *Close Encounters*, we recommend you use the *Overview of the book* section in this chapter to help you navigate. You might also be interested in other DPC outcomes such as the Practitioner Resource and peer-reviewed journal articles (details: www.education.exeter.ac.uk/dpc).

What happens when practitioners, teachers and university researchers enquire together?

Practical and theoretical background

DPC grew out of practical and theoretical discussions concerning the nature of creativity in dance and beyond, the relationship between creativity and performativity, and approaches to young people and partnership. The ways in which DPC findings could contribute to developing educational futures were also discussed.

The research specifically responded to a shared concern, pinpointed in 2007, that creativity in dance in secondary schools was suffering because of pressure from the testing and attainment agenda. From our experiences we felt this resulted in formulaic student choreography which lacked authenticity and originality. Perhaps more worryingly, even though dance had fought for its curriculum place, it was not always fulfilling its potential contribution, both to current education and to debates about what education might be (Ackroyd, 2001; Ofsted, 2006).

Alongside formulaic student choreography, we were all aware of pockets of highly innovative partnership practice being led by experienced dance artists and teachers working together on creative school projects. This practice was taking advantage of concurrent cultural and education policies which encouraged partnerships to foster student creativity (DCMS, 2006; Creative Partnerships, www.creative-partnerships.com). Our experience suggested that this renewed onus on partnership could offer a fruitful arena in which, through research, students' creativity could be re-connected with the creativity inherent in our art form. And so the DPC research project was born.

First, there was the question of what kind of creativity was occurring in dance partnerships. This originally became important because we were all involved in different capacities in facilitating creativity in educational partnership scenarios. We were all responding to requests to 'provide' creativity in schools. We queried whether our understanding of creativity was the same as that of the teachers, creative agents, artists, researchers and policymakers we were engaging with. We were keen to understand the unique contribution dance has to make to creativity in education, both now and in the future.

DPC team member Anna has argued that creativity is necessary because of uncertainty and intensification of change that characterises the twenty-first century (Craft, 2005; Craft, 2011). In Anna's work and that of other team members (Chappell, 2008; Rolfe *et al*, 2009) creativity is

What kind of creativity are we discussing and working with? Is it the same creativity that our colleagues are discussing?

about imagination and multiple possibilities, about shared generation of ideas, about immersion in the flow and about capturing unexpected and exciting new ideas. It is also creativity that sits within an ethical framework and requires wisdom (Craft *et al*, 2008).

On one level, we framed the DPC investigations using an explicit creativity conceptualisation, that of humanising creativity. This developed from Kerry's PhD study of creativity in primary level dance education (Chappell, 2008) and has proved useful in understanding creativity in other contexts (Chappell and Craft, in press). Although the university team have used this as their frame, other researchers have defined and conceptualised creativity as they see it. Importantly, it allowed all the researchers to express their own ideas.

Humanising creativity, developed in Chapter 7, builds on John-Steiner's (2000) criticisms of creativity as sited in the solitary thinker. The chapter emphasises that creativity happens individually, collaboratively and communally. Generative ideas emerge from embodied joint thinking and sustained, shared endeavours. Communal creativity is important to the humanising process and encourages a strong focus on empathy, shared ownership and group identity. The process is an emotional journey which is not always fun and involves conflict and difference. It is about becoming more humane, involving change and being aware of the consequences for other people (Chappell, 2008).

This conceptualisation sits alongside multiple current discourses on creativity which are evident in English creativity in education (Banaji, Burn and Buckingham, 2010). Humanising creativity chimes with democratic and political perspectives on creativity: creativity is seen as ubiquitous, a social good and as connected to play.

Three discourses which have varied in prominence across DPC are, however, in tension with humanising creativity and our general approach. The first is the idea of creativity as individualised, marketised, globalised and universalisable (identified by Craft and Jeffrey, 2001). This discourse thread represents anti-community, neo-liberal attempts to harness creativity in education to the economy. It stresses the constant generation of new ideas, lifestyles which rely on new consumption. Fashion dictates that constant change is a good thing and demands an 'observable product' (Craft, 2008a).

Secondly, DPC sits counter to educational performativity; the very reason that drove us to begin the research. We have argued (Chappell and Craft, in press) that there is a need to challenge the narrowing focus on achievement in core learning areas such as mathematics, English and science, and to question the link which is made between student performance and school rewards. Our aim is to avoid the potential superficiality inherent in harnessing creativity to performativity but rather to value creativity in its own right.

The third is the 'young people at risk' agenda. Identified by Craft (2011), this may be more of a threat. At one extreme in the continuum of Western world-views on the nature of youth is policy and accompanying practice which sees young people as at risk, vulnerable, passive and in need of adult supervision. This is arguably increasingly dominant in England. At the other end of the continuum, young people are treated as empowered, capable, active individuals who can be independent of adults. Our approach to creativity sits more naturally at this end. We are aware of the need to safeguard young people but challenge overprotective approaches.

DPC is about exploring the nature and development of co-participative partnership, and about acknowledging difference. We gained insight from a number of studies which situated partnership engagement as a version of 'apprenticeship learning' (eg Griffiths and Woolf, 2004). Other researchers (eg Galton, 2008) have dichotomised 'artist' and 'teacher'.

How do we work in partnership – through negotiation, polarisation or a particular combination of the two?

More pertinent to DPC is Jeffery's (2005) research into dialogic partnership engagement. His research with artists and performing arts teachers in a Further Education college produced a four-fold model of the teacher/artist relationship. It encompassed the shifting roles of teacher as artist, artist as educator, the artistry of teaching and artistic work as a model and educator. This laid the conceptual ground for our study, as the main emphasis was on how external and school partners co-produce partnerships. Our aim was to understand interaction and the ensuing creativity.

DPC positions itself in the area of alternative educational futures (Bussey and Inayatullah, 2008). We wished to explore how DPC might contribute to finding possible alternatives to policies and practices modelled on the industrial society of the Victorian era. What other ways of educating are possible?

What other ways of educating, relevant to adults and young people living in the 21st century, might DPC provoke?

The DPC research is thus embedded within discussions about the nature of creativity, interactions between creativity and performativity, attitudes to young people and partnership. We are exploring how findings in these areas might offer different educational futures to those which currently prevail.

Project aims

In researching creative partnerships in secondary dance education we aimed to open spaces in which to:

- catalyse pockets of innovation to develop creative practice in dance education and support more original student choreography
- enrich educational theorising of creativity, partnership pedagogy and accompanying research methodologies with dance education's unique contribution to this important theory-practice conversation
- make the positive outcomes of dance creative partnership practice understood and thus strengthen arguments for dance to be more centrally positioned within curricula
- position understanding from dance education to contribute to educational futures debates, specifically as a possible alternative way of working grounded in creative empowerment.

The DPC team believes that to investigate and develop creativity and partnership and meet our aims meaningfully, practitioners must be involved in all stages as resourced partner researchers. This has meant developing a methodology which embraces this stance. This methodology strongly informs the positioning and structure of the book.

Overview of the book

Close Encounters is written for a mixture of practitioners, researchers, academics, teachers, artists and students. Each author is a combination of these identities. We hope that the range of stories, voices and research lenses will be of interest.

Part 1, *Opening the space*, describes the DPC research background, rationale and methodology.

This chapter (1) relates the project's history; situates the research within the key theoretical areas of creativity, performativity, attitudes to young people, partnership and educational futures; and provides the navigational overview.

Chapter 2 by Anna Craft with Kerry Chappell, Linda Rolfe and Veronica Jobbins, details the methodology, specifically the mechanisms used to disrupt practice in order to produce research-focused spaces in which university and partner researchers could enquire together. It considers the challenges and achievements of this approach.

Part 2 of the book, *Catalysing practice: Learning from the partner researchers*, features the work led by the partner researchers in their sites. They write about enquiring into and developing their practice and about provoking others to develop practice in dance education and beyond. Each of the four chapters reflects the partner researchers' prior research experience, and the direction in which they felt comfortable to move. These written records of their work sit alongside their daily embodied practice.

In chapter 3, Bim Malcomson, Caroline Watkins with Linda Rolfe and Veronica Jobbins, investigate the roles and relationships in the London site in relation to power and ownership. They question and challenge views of how partnerships might work collaboratively in dance. They establish a desire to learn from each other as experienced professionals and from the pupils and show that this involves breaking the rules.

In Chapter 4, Abi Mortimer, Jackie Mortimer and Sian Goss with Linda Rolfe look at the relationship between collaborative choreography and creative engagement. The researchers in the South East site explore the importance to this relationship of imagery, ownership and feedback. Emphasising means not ends, the team identified questions for others to apply these ideas to their own practice.

In Chapter 5 Michael Platt, Kerry Chappell and Helen Wright, in the East of England site, reflect on de-constructing the teacher-artists' wisdom of practice within creative partnership. Which aspects of pedagogy ignite student learning? They argue for equality between the 'building blocks' of pedagogy and intuitive craft knowledge developed over years of experience. They look at this aspect of professionalism and the role of process within performativity agendas in teacher training, professional development and policy making.

Chapter 6, by Helen Angove and Rachelle Green with Kerry Chappell, is a dialogue between Helen and Rachelle reflecting upon their experience of a two year Dance for Health project. To what extent can notions of play be used by teachers and artists as a tool for creativity using the framing device of time, space and relationship? They explore the educational issues raised by seeing partnership practice through these lenses and offer ways of using play to facilitate creativity in planning, delivery and evaluation.

Part 3 of the book, *Creativity and partnership: but what kinds?* begins to position the research more theoretically. The research is synthesised across three of the sites to theorise the creativity and pedagogy within these studies of dance education partnership. The DPC methodology is examined and positioned within wider theoretical debates.

In Chapter 7, Kerry Chappell draws out the kinds of partnership and creativity evidenced within DPC and argues for creativity that is humanising, an embodied process of becoming which is mindful of its consequences. This creativity is grounded in a reciprocal relationship between the collaborative generation of new ideas and new identities, fuelled by dialogues between the participants and the world outside. Kerry argues that DPC offers an antidote to marketised and individualised creativity, to the performativity agenda and to notions of childhood at risk. She advocates ethically-guided creativity which is rigorous, risky and empowering and concludes that because humanising creativity is fundamentally embodied, it offers far greater shared hope for the future than the competitive sink or swim mentality which currently pervades our education system.

In Chapter 8 Linda Rolfe investigates some of the partnership approaches to teaching used by the external and school partners in the three sites and explores how they support pupils' learning. Dimensions of communities of practice (Wenger, 1998) are used to develop understanding of how the worlds of dance and education might overlap. Her findings point to ways of working that recognise the subtle differences that exist in practice instead of the common understanding so often assumed.

In Chapter 9, Anna Craft explores how the research-focused partnerships were characterised by 'meddling in the middle' (McWilliam, 2008) and how this helps explain how partners engaged in research-focused partnership. This recognised the role of uncertainty and not-knowing, acknowledged risk-taking, designing, assembling and editing together with university researchers while also acting as evaluators and critics. Anna explores how 'meddling in the middle' made the partnerships both dynamic and uncomfortable, and offered powerful potential for change. She argues that leaps made possible by partners who are curiosity-driven meddlers in the middle could overturn current (retrogressive) English policy.

Part 4 of the book, *From what is to what might be*, shifts the focus onto educational futures. The DPC findings strengthen arguments for dance to be more centrally positioned within curricula, and for positioning dance education so it can contribute to educational futures debates.

In Chapter 10, Veronica Jobbins looks at how some of the DPC creative partnerships have grown within, responded to and been challenged by the performativity agenda. Does dance only flourish if it successfully adapts to the demands and needs of the time? She argues that dance education has over 50 years' creative partnership practice expertise, so has much to offer the development of education. The chapter considers the DPC findings in relation to Smith-Autard's Midway Model for Dance Education and the need to attend to non-prescriptive creative dance experiences. Veronica concludes that unless dance is relevant to children and young people, it will have no pertinent meaning in schools.

In Chapter 11 Kerry Chappell and Anna Craft, with Linda Rolfe and Veronica Jobbins, synthesise the DPC findings in relation to the over-arching research question and consider the outcomes in terms of alternative educational futures. They pinpoint four current common educational concerns and how the DPC findings could contribute to responding to them. For the DPC university team this means reflecting on what education is for, and enacting changes via quiet cumulative revolution rather than grand revolt. They articulate the final layer of the DPC findings: a set of living principles of creative partnership which can assist in navigating beyond performativity and generating cumulative change. The chapter concludes that the need for on-going collective action through our combined potential as co-makers of our world is urgent if we are to secure rich educational futures.

This book seeks to intertwine the practical and the theoretical, and to make audible multiple researcher voices and perspectives. By presenting key thematic findings, theorising research-focused creative partnership and framing these in a methodological narrative, we hope to stimulate practice, research and policy both within and beyond dance education. We hope that this book will foster effective and exciting strategies and approaches for emergent, possible educational futures.

Note
1 Project number AH/F010168/1

2

Creating fruitful research spaces: methodology

Anna Craft with Kerry Chappell, Linda Rolfe
and Veronica Jobbins

...You just do what you do, you don't know what other people are doing, you only see the world through your own eyes don't you, so it's interesting to have these conversations ... (External partner South-East of England site, end of project)

Figure 2.1: DPC University researcher with partner researchers

This chapter focuses on the research methodology, particularly the mechanisms used to produce space for creative learning conversations as disruption to and development of practice. It explains the production of spaces through creative learning conversations to allow for multiple, exploratory but grounded conversations between researchers. Although difficult to achieve, these spaces allow for debate and difference and openness to action.

Partnership in enquiry

Dance Partners for Creativity (DPC) was established to develop and analyse space between creativity and performativity (see Chapter 1). We engaged in close-up partnership work to develop creativity, working in four sites across London, the South-East, East and South-West of England. Two schools involved in the sites held government-recognised Specialist Performing Arts status and one school was a School of Creativity. All the sites had in common a central focus on students aged 11-14 (Key Stage 3 in England).

Four enquiries

The structure of DPC involved four university-based researchers supported by six consultant research assistants and ten school-focused researchers[1]. Researchers were spread across four dance initiatives. In three of them collaboration was between school partner (an experienced teacher – most with dance specialism), external partner (with professional dance practitioner expertise) and university researcher (Kerry Chappell, Linda Rolfe, Anna Craft at Exeter University, and Veronica Jobbins at Trinity Laban) guiding the progress (see Figure 2.2 opposite).

In the fourth initiative in the South-West, the research developed differently. Two partner researchers worked in a variety of different external partner capacities within a large-scale partnership project, alongside one university researcher.

The project recognised that partner researchers might not view themselves as researchers, so offered resources to enable their participation. It prioritised development of a project-wide approach to research-focused creative partnership. Partners were encouraged to re-position themselves as researchers, listening to and actioning possibilities generated by the research.

While we initially considered including students as researchers, we decided after much deliberation that we did not have the research resources or time to genuinely engage students in this way. So while students' voices form part

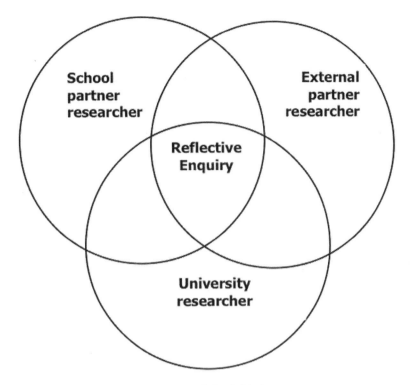

Figure 2.2: Research design in three of the initiatives

of the stories in this book, the research has focused its resource on facilitating adult practitioners into the researcher role.

Two layers of question

Two layers of research questions were explored across the study. The first was over-arching (and involved subquestions detailed in Chapter 11):

> *What kinds of creative partnerships are manifested between dance-artists and teachers in co-developing the creativity of 11-14 year olds in dance education, and how do they develop?*

Each group also developed their own specific research question in light of this main question.

> **London initiative**: How do the external partner and school partner work together; what are their roles and relationships?

> **South-East initiative**: How is creative engagement nurtured in partnership work and what does this mean for legacy?

East initiative: What aspects of pedagogical partnership practice make the 'magical moments' happen?

South-West initiative: Investigating the impact of time, space and relationship on how play might be used within the learning dynamic of a dance lesson

All were thus connected by the DPC umbrella research question. Because the South-West initiative developed differently with two external partner researchers, however, it did not contribute to responding to the umbrella question, answered in Chapters 7 to 10.

All four groups used creative learning conversations to develop their site-specific research strand through their own sub-question. In each site, research was negotiated and developed, guided by a generic pattern of involvement stretching across up to five school terms, open to local creative adaptation. The research was contingent on logistics, practices and the ideas of the partner researchers.

The four key partnership initiatives and research questions

London: At Dagenham Park School, Dance begins in the first year with 11-12 year olds having weekly hour-long practical lessons ranging from project work to cross curricular activity. The curriculum is designed to enhance students' understanding of technical, artistic and creative aspects of dance, encouraging them to become more confident critics and preparing them for examinations. It also promotes confidence, problem solving and communication skills underpinning a lifelong working ethos. Between the ages of 14-16, then 16-18, students are offered a variety of courses, from pure dance, to combined performing arts. The majority of those pursuing dance at 16+ progress to university to study dance. Some have now graduated, working as artists and educators.

The school offers a variety of enrichment opportunities, including:

- Gifted and Talented dance programme for 7-16 year olds
- Weekly dance training class ranging from ballet to contemporary dance including teachers from The Royal Ballet School and Trinity Laban
- 6th form Dance Academy, vocational style training provided by professional dance artists in collaboration with teachers

The school partner, Caroline Watkins and external partner Bim Malcomson (working for Dance Partnership Access at the Royal Ballet School) collaborated in DPC with Linda Rolfe and Veronica Jobbins (university researchers) to research roles and relationships in how they worked with one another.

South-East of England: Brockhill Park Performing Arts College (BPPAC) is an 11-18 comprehensive school, with Performing Arts status. For nearly 30 years BPPAC has offered Dance through school and Community Dance. In 2008 the school was awarded National School of Creativity (NSoC) Status. BPPAC has 5 full time dance teachers, including Sian Goss, school partner in DPC. The second school partner was Vice Principal Jackie Mortimer.

The partnership with Lîla Dance (local professional company) developed through formation of a youth dance company at Brockhill in 2006: The Mayakaras. The company of gifted and talented dancers, aged from 11-18, work with Lîla Dance to create new dance work. The project runs over 4-5 intensive 2 day periods within and beyond school. Lîla Dance Artistic Directors Abi Mortimer and Carrie Whitaker are involved in many community based projects/programmes. As well as developing and touring work, Abi and Carrie lecture at Chichester University.

Working with the Mayakaras enables Lîla Dance to investigate how their professional practice 'translates' to younger dancers. The collaboration allows work with young people free from timetabling, yet supported by staff, within a school where dance is celebrated and respected by students. The opportunity of working with Lîla Dance gives the Mayakaras a new experience outside the examination constraints, and thus to work with risk. It gives teachers a chance to reflect on practice.

Abi, Carrie, Sian and Jackie, in collaboration with university researchers Linda Rolfe and Veronica Jobbins, focused on researching: 'How is creative engagement nurtured in partnership work, and what does this mean for legacy?'

East of England: The research focused on partnership developed over several years between staff at the Local Education Authority Advisory Service, Holywells High School, its surrounding primary schools and local sixth form college. The project ran intensively for five weeks in early 2009 and culminated in an integrated performance involving over 70 students from the schools and college.

University researcher Kerry Chappell collaborated with partner researchers Michael Platt and Helen Wright. Helen was Joint Acting Head of Expressive Arts at Holywells, with responsibility for re-integrating Drama (her specialism) into the curriculum. She had previously worked in schools in Suffolk and Essex for 11 years, teaching 11-18 year olds Drama and Performing Arts.

Michael was a Learning and Teaching Adviser for Suffolk County Council's Inclusive School Improvement Service. His role included initiating, leading and evaluating arts projects in Suffolk schools.

Holywells High School in Ipswich is an 11-16 mixed comprehensive whose catchment largely comprises inner-city social housing. It is a challenging school. A few years previously it had been moved into special measures due to lower than average examination results. Much structured creative provision was then cut, resulting in the majority of students being starved of opportunities for creative expression. The research year was the first to involve students who had experienced Drama as integral to their weekly curriculum and therefore with growing awareness of performance etiquette.

Students aged 13-14 were invited to participate because of their enthusiasm or flair for creative work or because staff anticipated that they would garner social or confidence-building benefits. This resulted in a mixed ability group. During the project, school and college groups collaborated for four half days over four weeks at Holywells. On the fifth and final half-day all those involved came together to share their work. Partly as a result of this final session, the research question the partnership settled on was 'What aspects of pedagogical partnership practice make the magical moments happen?'

South-West of England: This initiative operated differently to other DPC enquiries, the DPC research being embedded within a bigger initiative. Step Change was a two-year dance and health project for Somerset which reached over 1,900 people. Between September 2008 and March 2010, 12 dance artists from Take Art worked with at least 60 dance groups in over 35 locations across the county. The project was conceived as part of a national drive to create healthier, more active communities by enabling people to take greater control of lifestyle choices. Participants were grouped into 5 strands comprising: children aged 5-14; young people aged 14-19; adults aged 20-50; people aged 50+ including the frail elderly; people with learning and physical disabilities.

Within Step Change, Helen Angove and Rachelle Green worked with a range of young people in schools and youth settings, in a variety of different partnerships. Advocating for the creation of environments which enabled participants to play, create and learn, their enquiry led them to reflect on their roles in the wider project. As dance artist, Helen drew on her previous background in schools to focus particularly on planning, delivery and evaluation of KS3 and 4 dance work through her own practice and also through the observations she undertook as peer mentor. Rachelle was the Project Manager for Step Change. Her work involved project teaching and learning evaluation with particular emphasis on identifying good practice and quality assurance procedures.

Ethics

Ethical relationships and procedures were carefully negotiated within the Exeter University Ethics Committee guidelines, which were in turn bound by the British Educational Research Association Ethical Code (2004). As indicated the project was committed to working co-participatively, so efforts focused on sharing understandings of the research and ethics involved. Confidentiality was at times in tension with visibility. Each partner brought to the research their own situated views on what might count as 'good' research. With so many dimensions to acknowledge, ethics were complex and under constant negotiation.

Beliefs about knowledge and consequent research design

Choosing sites, and framing the roles in each, was determined by the university team's commitment to an interpretive approach to knowledge, acknowledging the social construction of reality and multiple lived realities. This meant placing high value on understanding multiple perspectives, gathering data using a qualitative methodology where 'how' is a more salient question than 'how many'. By maintaining a close fit between our view of knowledge (epistemology) and what it means to 'come to know' (ontology) in the methods we used for data collection and analysis, DPC sought to be rigorous (Gavin, 2008).

The data collection and analysis process involved two layers, site and project level reflecting the two-layered questions. Analysis moved from site team to university researchers and research assistants for further consideration (discussed later in the chapter). Each stage was made transparent through a project-based website which showed the protocols and procedures, in an effort to maintain trustworthiness and quality (Lincoln and Guba, 1985) in terms of credibility, and dependability/confirmability. Endeavouring to make process transparent afforded opportunities for others to explore potential transferability in other contexts. So, although we were exploring unique partnership within dance education, we hoped our approach would offer opportunities for understanding educational partnership more generally. Overall, we were not seeking to claim 'objectivity'. We viewed realities as particular to social and cultural context, and to each individual participant.

Theory was built from coming to understand how meanings were interpreted by those involved in making them. We therefore set about constructing what we hoped would be open spaces for dialogue, in which every adult parti-cipant would contribute as co-participant researcher.

The study was informed by Critical Theory. We sought to develop theory oriented toward critiquing and changing, as opposed to theory oriented only toward understanding or explaining (eg McCarthy, 1991). It was distinct from purely socio-constructivist research, stretching far beyond researching *on* participants to researching *with* participants. We sought to change practice through researching. Dissemination of learning both within and beyond our research sites was therefore important in the research architecture.

Our approach to Critical Theory was mainly 'Celebratory' (de Souza Santos, 1999). In other words, we sought to develop a participatory approach with partner researchers involved in weaving research and practice together. This meant close communication. Bim, external partner in the London site, des-cribed the research at the project's end as:

> Going on a journey together, really massively. Supporting each other ... working together in a real way ... work[ing] out how you can feed off each other ... finding common ground and difference ... we found what was different and we cele-brated our difference ... we really explored things together. Sharing ideas and experience, we did ... listening ... finding out what the other wants, expects, needs ... Bim and Caroline spent a lot of time talking.

There was also an element of what de Souza Santos (1999) calls 'Oppositional' work. In each site we sought to transform site-based and wider practice and to influence policy in creative partnerships, starting with classroom or studio, as shown in this conversation between Linda, university researcher and Abi, external partner:

Linda:	Do you think that the way the research has been set up with this partnership ... it's actually influenced you ... ?
Abi:	Yes, I do.
Linda:	Can you expand on that?
Abi:	Yeah because it's just brought up questions and the questions are the things that you need to do to focus on what you've done, what you do well, what you could do better ... Questioning is at the heart of the process ... [and the] research process lets you see practice through other eyes
	(South-East England, end of project)

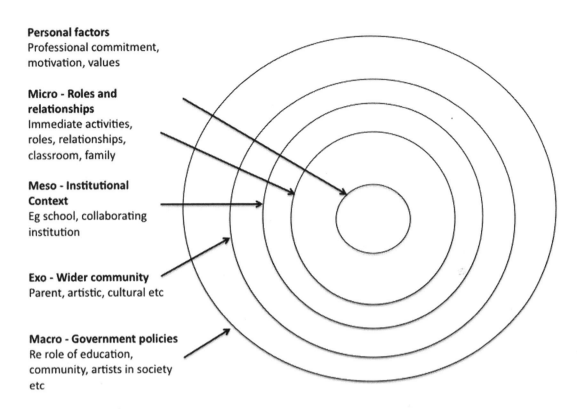

Personal factors
Professional commitment,
motivation, values

**Micro - Roles and
relationships**
Immediate activities,
roles, relationships,
classroom, family

**Meso - Institutional
Context**
Eg school, collaborating
institution

Exo - Wider community
Parent, artistic, cultural etc

Macro - Government policies
Re role of education,
community, artists in society
etc

*Figure 2.3: Ecological understanding of lived experiences in the project
(adapted from Bronfenbrenner)*

We hoped that as partners viewed their practice afresh, this would contribute to invigorating young people's creativity in their schools, but also, through dissemination and provocation, in new settings.

The many perspectives of external partners, school partners, university researchers and, in most sites, students, meant multiple levels of research. These are illustrated using Bronfenbrenner's (1979) 'ecological approach' to representing social action. His layered model shows local or immediate concerns nested within larger social and cultural environments.

This ecological approach is helpful in understanding the nature and role of creative learning conversations, occurring in the opened space between creativity and performativity. Influenced by Jonsdottir and MacDonald (2007) we adapted this model (Figure 2.3 above). DPC focused mainly on the three innermost layers, where the researchers' activities took place. We acknowledged and embraced the personal, working closely with 'roles and relation-

19

ships' in which participants were involved (those of dance partners and companies, departments, schools, and of different university partners). As teams made sense of their data, DPC also operated at 'institutional' level by encouraging dialogue and interplay between school and external partners and university researchers. Thus data collection and analysis occurred mainly in the first three layers. But DPC was also framed by wider social context and government policies.

The wider social context included: schools' own attitudes toward creativity in dance with 11-14 year olds, expectations of external and school partners of dance and the research process, and the research stance of university researchers. Each school, external partner and university researcher brought unique perspectives and values, although some overlapped. It was important in the research design to recognise this – one size would not fit all.

Government policies included curriculum policy for dance, national framing of and funding for creative partnership and wider research priorities of the national research funding body supporting the study. These two outermost layers of wider social context and government policies, framed work in dance at institutional level within each research site.

Perhaps most significantly this project was designed to nurture open dialogue. Influenced by Bakhtin (1984) and Lefebvre (1991), the DPC methodology evolved, into what we now refer to as 'living dialogic spaces' characterised by creative learning conversations.

Creative learning conversations in living dialogic space

These are highly reflective conversations based on evidence, with a focus on stimulating action. Creative learning conversations are active and reciprocal and therefore distinct from doing research on or to someone. As a consequence collecting and making sense of data has been dynamic, located in practice and experience, oriented toward change.

Data was generated through a range of provocation mechanisms designed to re-frame research space for powerful learning conversations. Examples include conceptual and journey mapping using visual media such as post-its, phrase completion exercises (eg 'Teacher is ... Artist is ... Partnership is ..., CapeUK, 2009), and graffiti work around student body outlines. Much mapping work generated visual media resources as a source and focus of discussion for researchers in each site (eg Figure 2.4 opposite).

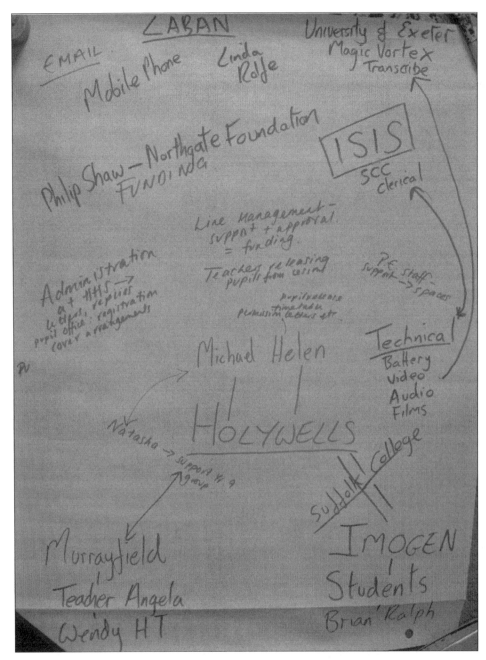

Figure 2.4 East of England site – partner researchers' first visual representation (start of project)

Figure 2.5: Discussion between university and partner researchers about visual data toward the end of the project

These maps, as featured in Figure 2.4 offered partner researchers ways to represent and engage in conversation about *how they saw things*. Each map therefore represented a partial view. In every site partner researchers mapped together at least twice, comparing the current with the previous. All conversations were audio-recorded and transcribed. Repeated mapping and discussion allowed for and captured representations and ideas shifting over time. Figure 9.2 in chapter 9 shows the final conceptual map, created by the East of England partners.

Mechanisms used later for analysing and representing ideas within learning conversations included: shape-puzzles, photographic montage, conversation-style conference presentations (modelled on Bannerman, 2004). Also included were filmed conversations based on layers of previous analysis between research teams members (eg Figure 2.5 opposite).

DPC also made use of traditional qualitative methods such as interviews, fieldnotes, observations, photography and film.

Guiding Principles in living dialogic space

Given our interpretive view of knowledge and consequent orientation toward qualitative work, and our oppositional critical theory intention, the following principles were emphasised. In keeping with our participatory perspective, they lean toward emancipation and empowerment.

- Change is generated from practice (rather than by external forces)
- Verbalisation and embodiment of change is valued
- Cyclical re-visiting is encouraged, since learning conversations develop over time
- Personal and partial perspectives are inherent and expected
- Meaning is neither transparent nor truthful through representation alone
- Interpretation too offers only a partial representation
- Dialogue and conversation cast light on multiple perspectives
- The goal is not to find one uniform answer to research questions but to share multiple perspectives on these
- It is important to communicate the findings synthesised through the conversations to the researchers' peers in ways that are credible and valuable
- The process of engagement in creative learning conversations may involve disagreement and conflict, or reveal irreconcilable differences

Figure 2.6: Analysis during the first whole-group triangulation of whole-project
research question

- Despite efforts toward equality and openness, creative learning conversations may nevertheless involve inequalities in participation, since creative learning conversations are located in wider power structures of each setting.

How we collected and analysed data was therefore intended to capture and explore multiple perspectives. The analytic process involved all university and partner researchers and some research assistants (depending on role), in making meaning – a hermeneutic process (LeCompte and Preissle, 1993) which we sought to apply through layers of analysis for each question level (site and whole-project). At both levels of question, we worked through comparative analysis from 'open coded/free thinking' analysis of data to identification of data-saturated themes. We strove to include triangulation of data, and where possible, of analyst. In each site, partner researchers worked with university researchers on site level questions. For project-level questions university researchers worked together drawing in partner researchers on key whole-group occasions (Figure 2.6 opposite) later extended by research assistant Debbie Watson undertaking overall (filmed) triangulation with university researchers .

We found Sparkes (2009) helpful. He recognises the need for qualitative researchers to make 'informed, principled and responsible decisions' (p301), and for constant re-interpretation of research data in construction of represented meanings. Meaning-making was frequently challenging, Helen, a school partner researcher at the East of England site, observed at the start of the project:

> I said to Kerry today well she's making me think about me more than I thought I was going to have to, which is really interesting.

We were acutely aware of the risk of unintentionally disempowering participants by being overly rational or critical in style (Ellsworth, 1989). We therefore sought to develop a dynamic and changing space for interaction, in the research process and in learning and teaching in the dance studio.

From 'fixed and closed' to 'flexible and open'

Creative learning conversation principles are oriented toward co-actioning change. Learning conversations nurtured in DPC reflect transition from what Lefebvre (1991) refers to as 'absolute' (fixed, unchanging, closed) perspectives, through 'abstract' (boundaried, disjunctive, hierarchical) approaches, to 'differential' ones (open counter-space of flexibility, enabling differences to be heard and recognised).

The shift from fixed to flexible approaches in the living dialogic space of creative learning conversations was largely located at *institutional* or school level. At this level DPC explored personal and institutional values and inherent tensions and continuities. It was at school level where the greatest tensions in living dialogic space were experienced. Here we saw the external frame of social and policy perspectives literally in dialogue with individuals' values.

Lefebvre's ideas emphasise inherent potential for conflict and difference, highlighting latent fragility and balance inherent in creative learning conversations. Yet the orientation of learning conversations toward action, and thus change, also signals evolutionary potential for developing shared creative approaches (Chappell and Craft, in press).

As the project unfolded, so did our lived and theoretical understanding of creative learning conversations. Embodied, emotionally charged and physically and intuitively expressed in a highly personal way through dialogue, they focused on change. By highlighting the dialogic dimension, we emphasise their dynamic, multiple and open character at institutional (ie school and external practitioner) level, drawing on roles and relationships (immediate, classroom level, experiences and values) and thus the personal. Creative learning conversations sought to acknowledge and make space for possible difference and even conflict. Efforts were made to reveal visible social values (including funding and priorities in relation to creative partnership in dance) and shifting policy frameworks in our conversations.

Tensions in the methodology

The model of living dialogic space brings challenges. In making visible multiple influences of institutional, wider social values and government policies as experienced in roles and relationships, tensions are highlighted. Whilst open space encouraged multiple perspectives, increasing pressures on institutional, wider social values and government policy systems pressed toward unitary performativity. These tensions were manifest in:

- experiences, values and identities of different partners as co-researchers, and
- wider environment and values around creative partnership in dance.

Bringing diverse perspectives to the surface in a truly democratic and open way is always complex, given the inherent power relationships embedded in wider social structures which are reproduced in specific institutions and relationships. We were acutely aware, for example, of the power imbalance inherent in the fact that the university team developed the idea, held the budget and invited partner researchers to participate. Each participant brought a unique pattern of expertise and confidence in doing research. This translated into distinctive ways in which participatory involvement were manifest in each site, reflecting the underpinning power, authority and empowerment.

The wider parts of the ecological system in which DPC enquiries were developing, are themselves dynamic and therefore changing. As the project entered its final phase of analysis a change of government brought in a coalition between Conservative and Liberal Democrat politics and thus a new wider social context to the educational system and new government policies with much greater emphasis on formal aspects of curriculum, learning and assessment.

The DPC methodology in a changing policy context

Research-focused professional development appeared to be taking a back seat as the new government promised 'radical reform' (DfE, 2010:4) and moved away from capability toward core knowledge (apparently excluding the Arts). Yet, as the following chapters show, whilst the emergent New Basic approach to educational development has the potential to stifle living dialogic space, the opposite has developed in DPC. The DPC methodology aspires to an emancipatory and bottom-up character, despite the apparent emphasis of the new political regime on narrower outcomes for education. Such research may prove fruitful in the long term, not only for those directly involved in this research project but for others who are inspired by it.

The commitment of the new regime to diversity of provision may possibly bring refreshed opportunities for research-focused, living dialogic spaces for developing educational futures. This is explored further in Part 4 of the book.

Note
1 University researchers: Anna Craft, Kerry Chappell, Linda Rolfe, Veronica Jobbins. Research assistants: Margo Greenwood, Chu-Yun Wang, Linda McConnon, David McCormick, Debbie Watson, Maria Gregoriou. Partner researchers: Helen Angove, Sian Goss, Abi Mortimer, Jackie Mortimer, Carrie Whitaker, Rachelle Green, Bim Malcomson, Michael Platt, Caroline Watkins, Helen Wright.

PART TWO
CATALYSING PRACTICE:
LEARNING FROM THE PARTNER
RESEARCHERS

3

The 'double act' of partnership, breaking the rules to explore new possibilities for dance pedagogy

Bim Malcomson and Caroline Watkins
with Linda Rolfe and Veronica Jobbins

What happens between two very experienced dance professionals as they work in partnership, one the internal school partner and the other the external artist, as they investigate their roles and relationships? How are their roles defined and what can the partners learn from each other in the situation?

Bim: I think what is happening in this project is ... It's making me question what an artist's role is and what a teacher's role is.

(partner and university researchers, London site, beginning of project)

This is one of the questions Bim, Artist in Education at the Royal Ballet School, and Caroline, Head of Dance at Dagenham Park School, focused on within their Dance Partners for Creativity (DPC) initiative when they explored new possibilities for dance educators. This chapter documents their experiences in the London site and the ways in which they managed to form an exceptionally close collaborative working partnership. How the project contributed to the creative dance work of students as they move from Year 8 to Year 9 is explored in the context of Dagenham Park Church of England School.

This fully inclusive state school gained Arts College status in 2002 and has undertaken many collaborative projects including research into creativity for the Specialist Schools and Academies Trust (www.ssatrust.org.uk). Dagenham Park has successfully forged partnerships with The Royal Ballet School, Trinity

Laban and The Royal Academy of Dance, offering opportunities for both its dance staff and the students to enrich their learning and develop as creators and educators. The university researchers were Veronica Jobbins, Head of Professional and Community Development, Laban, and Linda Rolfe, Senior Lecturer in Education at the University of Exeter.

Context

This research project involved Caroline, the school partner, and Bim, the external partner, working with two year 8 dance classes, each with twenty four boys and girls, aged 12-13 years. It began in the second half of the summer term and continued into the first half of the autumn term. This was deliberately designed to explore the differences in attitudes or application frequently observed in year 9 pupils, who sometimes return after the summer vacation with their self-confidence undermined by their rapid physical and emotional development. The dance content of the project was not esta-blished at the outset and part of the challenge for Bim and Caroline was to define what and how they would teach in partnership over the lessons.

They dedicated time to talking together before and after every teaching session and their reflective conversations became a significant source of data. The university researchers were involved in regular lesson observations, making field notes and conducting interviews with Bim and Caroline. Caroline arranged to have each lesson and the pupil interviews filmed to capture their comments about their thoughts on the lessons both visually and in writing. Discussions were planned in so the research team could reflect on the direction the project was taking and how best to capture the ethos of the partnership. This comment of Caroline's set the tone of the project:

> Right from the beginning we established that ... we're going to break the rules, we're not going to have the confinement of the curriculum ...

Her statement reflects the openness, trust and confidence they had in the power of their relationship both to 'fuel their passion' and to take the students' work to another level.

Caroline's viewpoint:

As Head of Department it is my duty to ensure that the needs of my team of three staff and a cohort of approximately twelve hundred students are met. I recognise that there are ever changing trends in teaching which need to be reflected in our practice, such as a greater emphasis on student led activity. Whilst this has always been at the centre of creativity, there is a pressure in schools for students to experience a fulfilling and enriching education that engages them and promotes their academic development.

Bim's viewpoint:

When working with young people I feel that it is my job to encourage them to find their own voice and to make an environment where they can stretch their own borders creatively. I also think it is important to have high expectations so that each individual aspires to work to their full potential.

Early thoughts about the partnership
Fear of the unknown
Caroline:

As a teacher with many years of experience, I have sometimes found it difficult to establish a successful creative project with artists and outside agencies. Unless you dedicate time to researching the practitioner or company and planning the focus and projected outcomes together, how can you know if the artist is right for your students and that the experience will be purposeful and educationally sound? Secondly, how can you establish trust in the relationship with the artist and manage the roles as they develop throughout the project?

Bim and I realised that we had a unique opportunity to share a focus and engage in a collaboration which would examine our roles. We began by reflecting on our individual roles as an artist and a teacher. I was not surprised to discover that there were discrepancies between what we believed were typical perceptions of each other's roles. However, when asked to illustrate where we felt we featured at the project start we drew very similar pictures placing ourselves at either side of the children (Figure 3.1 overleaf).

Questioning our roles
Caroline:

Time became an enormous factor in developing our relationship. The opportunity to discuss openly and honestly throughout our collaboration often became as exciting as the practical sessions. We agreed that we would not have a finished polished performance. I was keen to break the rules and seek 'the many different ways we can' aspect in order to explore creativity fully and develop new ideas and confidence in the students. I asked questions such as: how did Bim feel about this way of working as opposed to creating a piece in her usual working context? Was this to be a limiting experience for her? What did she bring to the project? I was both excited by the opportunity to push myself into new areas of teaching, and also fearful that

Figure 3.1: Bim and Caroline's first project illustrations

perhaps Bim would think I would not stand up to the challenge. Bim and I agreed to share equal responsibility and aimed to challenge preconceived ideas by opening ourselves up to new avenues and take what was at first, a very awkward and painful journey into what became the most exciting and rewarding project I have ever engaged in.

Bim:

As an artist going into schools, the project objectives are usually to create a final dance piece of a high standard that will be performed, and to have an engaging educational process. Working in this way the teacher usually supports me throughout the project and I lead the sessions. Caroline and I began the project following the conventional model, with me mainly leading the sessions and her in support. But we kept coming back to the question: 'How does our relationship affect the student's creativity?' Because this question was posed by us again and again, it encouraged us to look at how we interacted in the classroom and what our roles were both in the planning and execution of the project.

Deconstructing and rebuilding roles and relationships
Relationships and trust
Caroline:

We needed to address why there is often a perceived hierarchy between an artist and teacher. Is it because the artist is responsible for the success of the creative outcome or because they have their name on the credits? In my experience, many artists refer to a toolbox of creative tasks which are tried, tested and safe – but some fail to challenge and inspire the teacher and students. This is usually due to the lack of time invested in the advance planning of the project. Discovering what the children have previously learnt, understanding the vision of the dance teacher and taking time to discuss how best to facilitate new experiences for the children, are all keys to a successful partnership.

Dropping the usual curriculum and exposing the children to new and exciting creative possibilities was risky. Neither Bim nor I knew how we were going to achieve this. In our weekly discussions we took turns to think like the other and present ideas both conventionally and unconventionally. In the dance studio we gradually relinquished our initial awkward state of power and control to become equals. This was not an easy journey. At times Bim would pass the control to me, having laid the foundations for something really gritty that required me to expose myself to the children and made me feel awkward. Bim's exuberant personality had to be matched! Our playful explorations together frequently led to me being spontaneously lifted upside down or overpowered bodily, which of course I had to challenge. The children saw me drop my usual teacher persona and, convinced by the double act that we eventually became, they were inspired as explorers, parallel to Bim and I. Their learning was taking a new direction. Their confidence boosted, the children became more demanding of each other. Their skills of communication were tested as they became more confident leaders and creators.

When I asked, 'What have you learnt from working with Bim and me?', this is what one child replied: 'I've learnt how to dance openly and freely and how to explore new ideas without feeling embarrassed'.

The sessions were fast paced and the children had to think and react instantly, as did we. We trusted each other to challenge our ideas in the studio even if we were not confident about what could be learnt from it or where it would lead. We were brave enough to refine each other's ideas at a moment's notice, frequently passing over the control to each other. We were committed to the partnership developing creatively, committed to the success of the relationship evoking new confidence in the children, and that meant being brave enough to trust what we had to bring to the creative environment.

We were frequently working side by side quite literally as the photograph shows.

Figure 3.2: Bim stands to the left of Caroline as they face the class

The roles developed

Bim:

In my normal life I am a dance artist and a teacher. I was asked to come into the partnership as an artist. This proved to be interesting, as being an artist meant I was not being a teacher in any way, thus in the first few classes I did not draw on any of my teaching skills or strategies. This was, of course, a disaster, as the students were not being well managed by me, which resulted in many pupils becoming un-motivated and some behavioural issues arising. What was brilliant about this rather unfortunate misunderstanding at the beginning was that it really made Caroline and me question 'What is an Artist?' and 'What is a Teacher?' and we made lists of what these roles meant to us (figures 3.3a and 3.3b overleaf). This is supposing the two are different, because actually most of us are teachers *and* artists.

Having deconstructed these roles we could then decide what we wanted to bring to the project. I wanted Caroline to take more responsibility for the creative ideas as the project developed, because who says teachers are not good choreographers? The disciplining and running of the class became more like a fluid double act rather than me being stuck in the so-called artist role with Caroline as the teacher. Pulling these stereotypical roles apart gave us the freedom to rethink and make our own version of what we wanted to be. Here I have a rather embarrassing confession, but it is important to share it! A reading (Jeffery, 2005) we were given at the start of the project had a huge impact on my approach. The author suggested that artists ask themselves: 'What can I learn from a teacher?' This hit me like a light bulb going on. In all the years I have been doing projects in schools I have never thought about this. How arrogant is that? The model below is typical when an artist goes into a school:

Artist

Teacher

For some reason a hierarchy exists with the artist on top and the teacher acting in a supportive role to meet the artist's needs. Though this way of working is valid and possibly productive it is not the only way. Having identified the model normally used we asked ourselves questions and created our own working model:

Artist   Teacher

Whilst saying this is not the only way, it is important that we question roles and models to create our own ways of working with artists, teachers, colleagues and young people.

Figures 3.3a and b: Artist teacher role thinking

Collaboration

At the end of the project, when discussing what collaboration meant to Bim and Caroline with regard to their journey we came up with the following:

- Collaboration is coming together to share ideas in order to create a purposeful and successful project.
- Working in partnership means we work together as equal partners to ensure the delivery is cohesive.
- Collaboration means learning from and being open to the other.
- Collaboration demands dropping certain things, mainly control in this instance, to enable new ways of working and unexpected things to happen.

As the project developed we discovered that we let go of huge amounts of power and control to work in collaboration: as the artist I had to allow for other peoples' artistic voice and vision. As the teacher working within the school curriculum Caroline had to forsake certain learning outcomes. Now let's face it, relinquishing power and working in new ways is quite painful! I am not going to pretend this was an easy task for either of us, but the outcome, once we had gone through the pain threshold and committed to going on a journey, was astonishing.

Reflection and implications
Roles and relationships

Caroline:

Being brave was a key factor throughout this project. I was faced with having to challenge my creative and artistic ability, and also my personality in front of the children. I also had to be brave enough to let go of the curriculum and allow the students to learn through new and sometimes unconventional methods. Would they learn the terminology and apply it to their problem solving tasks without the usual explanation and layering? The answer is yes. Often thrown in at the deep end, the students still managed to expand their ideas and take ownership of their learning.

This was particularly evident when the class was divided into two groups and one student in each group volunteered to be the 'artist'. They became more confident to challenge their peers to explore ideas and improvise through this experience of directing the group.

Bim:

It was apparent to the students that Caroline and I were on a creative journey together. We were taking risks in our practice and being brave. We worked closely together physically and demonstrated creative explorations and co-teaching in what ended up as quite an amusing double act. This was hugely inspirational for the students as we were evolving a creative environment. Through our successful working relationship we were positive role models for the students which was reflected in their work. I think being brave was and is essential. Being creative in any shape or form, whether making a dance piece or exploring new ways of working, demands bravery. It takes you into unknown territory where exciting new things can emerge and develop.

Caroline:

We constantly asked questions which explored our beliefs and experiences. This challenged and inspired the pupils, affecting their working relationships. A student who rarely brought his kit and was never at the front of the class as a leader, became concerned about his progress, asking me to discuss his next lesson. By taking responsibility for shared practical responses he became more confident and able to voice his ideas. He was recognising and echoing the way in which Bim and I presented ourselves in the partnership.

Is a performance outcome implicit/integral in a dance lesson?
Caroline:

At Dagenham Park lessons across the curriculum are planned with a similar structure: Connect/Explore/Try/Review/Anticipate.

Lessons have learning phases to facilitate teaching and learning in which the students share, discuss and give feedback on their ideas. Through the use of assessment criteria they reach their learning targets, improve and make progress. Teacher and student modelling of exemplary work is essential to raise expectations and set a climate for achievement and success.

Familiarity with routine procedures seems necessary for a successful one hour lesson which includes changing into practical clothing. But with several lesson phases is this enough time to be creative? With two successive classes there was no opportunity for Bim and me to reflect between each session. At times this hindered my introduction to the second session, but time to refocus from teacher in the changing room to artist/teacher collaborator in the studio happened when Bim took the register.

We swapped roles as leaders during the teaching and sometimes became learners with the students. Unfortunately we made a vital mistake in trying to create a sharing of students' dance work in the last session. Bim and I agreed the artistic vision for the structure of the work. However, in order for this to be successful and for both classes to achieve their performances in time, we had to separate into two studios. For the first time Bim and I were working alone.

The atmosphere changed in both studios as the students worked towards their final presentation. Their ability and confidence to perform diminished due to the lack of time and a fear of the unknown. The students were presented with a new set of choreographic tools which they had to explore under timed conditions. Their prior learning with us had taken them on an exciting journey of self discovery and creativity. However, at no time in the past had we explored how to structure their work into a finished performance. In this situation I felt the need to teach dance material to groups of individuals. The students became confused as sections of work became disjointed and overlapped with their original material. Their dance was being directed to become something else and this was an approach that we had set out to challenge.

For the first time Bim and I were working alone and it felt wrong. We had become creative equals who shared and promoted a double act which inspired students to work together. Now the students disagreed with how we took the lead in each group. We had each become the director, choreographer, mentor and disciplinarian. As the students work was changed they had little opportunity to contribute to the structure of the dance which promoted a feeling of negativity. Some were disappointed that the work was no longer their own. Bim and I were greatly affected by this as it felt damaging for the students and was not what we had anticipated. We would have worked in a different way had we decided at the beginning to share work, rather than this last minute decision to bring the students together to perform.

How Bim changed her role with the pupils and directed their work in order to achieve a performance is described in these field notes written by the university researcher at the close of the project:

> Bim slips into 'choreographer' mode, different from where she has been teacher/facilitator in the students' creativity. Instead she starts directing the groups and re-arranging the movement material but she does not explain this shift in her role to the students or why she is making the decisions. They are cross about this as the students clearly have ownership over their dance material but seem to accept Bim's role as it becomes evident what she is doing.
>
> Bim is not letting students in on her creative decision making.
>
> Group 2 in the middle starts with a girl's duet. Bim stops the group before they have finished and asks another pair to start their sequence so that their movement will overlap with the original duet. The students do not like this, they say to Bim, 'that's not our sequence', she responds and says, 'it's OK you will do your sequence, they reply, 'Miss, you are changing it'.

Bim replies 'It's just repetition, no big deal, I am just playing around with it!'

Bim carries on directing the group, changing the use of space and telling them when to run on.

Boys at the back do not understand where to come in, Bim directs and rehearses. Bim clicks fingers, no use of music.

Bim commented on this situation after the project was completed:

I think there was confusion at the end of the project about suddenly having to conform to certain conventions, that is a performance of some kind, that we had clearly not been following and was not the point of this project. If the object of the project had been to have a final performance then the students would not have had the experience they did in the last session.

This questions the different teaching methodology required when the emphasis is on the product and performance of work as opposed to creativity and a journey involving abstraction and imagination.

What was learnt?

Bim and Caroline:

The DPC project provided space to allow for the exploration of roles and relationships which evolved in the partnership. Using her creativity in a different way allowed Bim to work with Caroline in exploring new models of practice. For Bim it meant letting go of her ego and giving space to the teacher's and young people's voices. The young people became empowered to collaborate as they were intrigued by the relationship between the partners and themselves. There was freedom to explore ideas when the focus on a performance outcome was removed, and for Bim this created a very different situation from normal.

The success of the partnership was founded upon investing time to discuss the skills, interests and needs of the pupils. This, together with commitment and vision, are important factors to consider in future projects. Bim and Caroline constantly questioned each other and themselves to discuss how 'rules' could be broken and then re-established.

What is new in the partnership?

To create new ways of working and challenge preconceived ideas involves a shift in thinking about partnership. DPC has demonstrated that a variety of models or ways of working are needed. Partners need to be clear about their roles and intentions for the partnership in order to nurture young people's creativity in dance. It is thus necessary to identify where the power in the creative process resides.

Figure 3.4: Young people encouraged to share work in progress

Creating an artistic vision is often thought to be wholly the role of the artist. Young people explore and produce work but have no ownership of the product as this rests with the artist. This view was questioned and challenged by the partners and students.

The creative relationship developed between Caroline and Bim is one that could be replicated between a teacher and a group of young people in school by:

- building trust
- allowing another person to contribute ideas
- valuing others ideas
- negotiating leadership, with power and control going back and forth

Different models allow people to create ways of working that are appropriate to the creative situation. Both partners set out to break the rules and challenge ideas which they had previously accepted as part of their practice. Through DPC they started to question and rewrite the rules. This gave them insights into how their relationship might affect the students' creativity. They recognised how important it was for them to work as equals and actively collaborate with each other and the class. This is part of a process which they continue to develop in their own professional roles.

4
Embracing collaborative choreography on the path to creative engagement

Abi Mortimer, Jackie Mortimer and
Sian Goss with Linda Rolfe

Figure 4.1: The Mayakaras in a performance of 'How to Handle Interruptions Graciously' (2009)

Genuinely engaging a group of young people in a collaborative and collective creative process is challenging. This chapter focuses on how Lîla Dance achieved this with a student dance company, The Mayakaras.

It explores how the collaborative process of choreography helped inform understanding of pupils' creative engagement. The research was carried out during 2009 at Brockhill Park Performing Arts College (BPPAC) in Kent, an 11-18 comprehensive school, with Performing Arts status in the Dance Partners for Creativity (DPC) South East site. The research team was made up of partner researchers Abi Mortimer and Carrie Whitaker (the Artistic Directors of Lîla Dance, a professional performance company based in the South-East and a creative associate of The Point, Eastleigh), Sian Goss, one of the school's dance teachers, Jackie Mortimer, Deputy Head and former Head of Dance at the school, and selected students, with university researcher, Linda Rolfe, Senior Lecturer at the University of Exeter.

We began by discussing the possible research question. This centred around the school's interest in what made this partnership in dance such a successful learning environment for students. The questioning journey finally led to the question: how is creative achievement or engagement nurtured in partnership work?

The research process entailed gathering information through conversations, interviews, and reflective commentaries about The Mayakaras project. Conceptual drawings were used to prompt thinking and communicate ideas visually. Photographic and video evidence was collected and used to document the process and record the final performance. Linda, the university researcher, first drafted an outline of how the research process might work and this was shaped by the partner researchers as the project progressed so they could manage their time most effectively. As the project took place over a series of intensive weekends, it became evident that more time was needed to allow for reading transcripts and collecting additional information from students through interviews and visual mapping activities. The data analysis was shared amongst the research team at BPPAC, with Linda leading on the cycles of detailed constant comparative analysis.

Following details of the context below (for further information see Chapter 2), this chapter takes the perspective of Abi Mortimer of Lîla Dance as a starting point for comment and interjection from dance teacher, Sian Goss. Sian builds on Abi's perspective by providing insight into how the partnership reaches deeper into the school environment. Jackie Mortimer, Deputy Head and former Head of Dance, contributes her reflections from a whole school perspective.

The partnership between BPPAC and Lîla Dance

This partnership developed through the formation of a youth dance company at Brockhill in 2006 called The Mayakaras. The company of gifted and talented dancers, aged from 11 to 18, work each year with Lîla Dance on the creation of a new dance work. The project runs over four or five intensive two-day periods both in and out of school hours. Working outside school hours has given staff at the school a chance to consider the effectiveness of extended school provision, and its value in contributing to learning. The realisation of each commission is achieved through collaboration between student, teacher and practitioner (Lîla Dance). All parties share a common vision and the aim to drive work into new territory while striving for a high level of excellence.

The Mayakaras is made up of Brockhill/Instep members and the selection process for the Company is facilitated by the teachers in partnership with Lîla Dance. Instep are a Youth Dance Company which is based at the school but which serves the community. They offer dance opportunities to a wide and eclectic community of dancers, ranging from pre-school to the over 40s. It was at Instep that we first experimented with a mixed age group and it was this that led to the decision to create The Mayakaras.

Teachers invite students to join the project whose ability to sustain focus and work creatively has been recognised through regular classes. Lîla Dance also choose dancers through attending dance events at the school. Technical ability, although important, is not the sole criterion for inviting students into the company. Lîla Dance is interested in the whole dancer – their focus, energy, ability to accept feedback and willingness to work within a team.

Each year, new members are selected, as The Mayakaras lose school leavers but gain new members from the lower years. This is important as the new dancers enter an environment that already has a mode of behaviour and a philosophy established by Lîla Dance with The Mayakaras. The more experienced members of the company become role models for the new members, who in turn will become mentors for new members in years to come.

The creative process

Abi Mortimer:

The following subheadings break down Lîla Dance's practices into three strands. All the strands focus on using the creative process as a means to foster creative engagement with young people. The processes are all entwined and each carries implications for the others. When exploring the ideas practically I would expect many of the processes to occur simultaneously, but for the sake of explanation this section is divided into three core strands: Imagery, Ownership and Feedback. This attempts to explain the particular way that Lîla Dance approach choreography, using the terminology as we specifically use it in this context.

Imagery

What do we mean by an image? In our practice an image is an idea that is planted into the body and mind to trigger a human response, be it emotional, physical or intellectual. The emphasis is always on the intrinsic relevance of the image so that the young person understands the movement they generate from a kinaesthetic point of view. An image could be evoked from a number of sources, such as visual stimuli, music/sound, or the use of language. The latter is particularly important to the process Lîla Dance adopts in fostering creative engagement, as particular use of language affects the teaching style itself.

The use of imagery refers to the practice of constructing imaginative and personal connections to the movement material. This has complex and exciting implications for young people, whose imaginations are often boundless! In Lîla Dance's work with The Mayakaras, imagery has become the key vehicle by which we aim to nurture creative engagement. Why? Because it is a means to evoke a response that is unique but above all is meaningful to each individual. For example:

> A: Sit down, cross legged. Go to place your hand on the floor, but do so with a slow and steady pace and with a steady hand. Reach with your fingertips. The moment your fingers touch the floor, pull your hand away in a direct line and with speed.

> B: Sit down, cross legged. Imagine the floor is covered in hot coals, go to touch it. What would your reaction be?

A causes a cognitive response through following instructions that explain what and how to do a specific movement. B provides the possibility for a more personal response, as an image is evoked through the choice of language that recalls movement memories. The response from B is also evoked through using less words, it is immediate and powerful because it speaks to knowledge already held in the body. By using an image, emphasis is placed on the 'why' and 'how' of the movement and this in turn informs how the movement itself is perceived and understood. The movement response therefore feels like it comes from the self as it is personal.

Jackie Mortimer:

The Mayakaras use imagery in their lessons and when offering feedback to peers. This has significantly improved the quality of classroom work. This is illustrated by the Year 13 (aged 17 to 18) Advanced Level examination dance group which contained seven Mayakara members. Part of the syllabus focused on creating a work with an original perspective based on Mats Ek's *Giselle*.

The choreographic process took place over several months and was accomplished through observing themes and ideas in the dance and then setting tasks. Teachers and Mayakara members regularly used imagery as part of the creative process and in the final stages of rehearsal, enabling all the cast members to re-connect with the intention behind the movement material.

At Key Stage 3 the process is equally valuable and the quality of students' engagement is apparent in lessons. For example, in response to task setting we notice students' language moving away from action words, 'do this and then this', into qualitative and expressive language, 'it feels like this; melt, shiver, recover'.

Sian Goss:

The use of imagery is embedded in dance lessons and is now being explored in more depth by teachers. The students involved have been able to take their experiences into their curriculum work, which can positively influence their learning and confidence. This is evident in the following comments made by the youngest two members of The Mayakaras:

> In dance lessons, it might not be like the same material but ... we bring back the task, like when we're working in groups in class you won't say oh yeah this is what we did in The Mayakaras, but we know ... that's a task we were given and that made good material.

> I think we bring back our confidence as well, because after the Mayakaras sessions we go away and we feel a lot more confident working with other people.

Imagery leading to engagement and challenge
Abi Mortimer:

When teaching movement phrases or sequences to The Mayakaras we use imagery in our language. This has a particular effect when learning movement from one body to another. This transfer of movement can feel foreign, but imagery makes a connection where the dancer is able to take ownership over the material. Images help with the translation from the outside to the inside, the copying can cease and internal understanding and interpretation begin. If used effectively, imagery can make learning sequences a creative and interpretive act which requires imagination and engagement.

Jackie Mortimer:

Observing Lîla Dance work in this way opened up a debate about the value of this approach for Key Stage 3 students, (aged 11 to 14), who we tended to teach in a didactic way. We wanted students to feel challenged but also have a voice in the way their work develops. We try to offer a balance between technical correctness and creativity. Movement stemming from a task or an image may lack technique but say much more about the individual, and for that reason communicate more powerfully.

Abi Mortimer:

Case study: Glass of Water

I taught The Mayakaras a technical phrase that focused on the use of core strength, alignment and plié to achieve a smooth and controlled action in and out of the floor. To achieve an understanding of this I used the image of 'a suspended glass of water' in the tummy. I then discussed what parts of the phrase required control and lift of the torso to 'protect and look after the water level in the glass', and when the water might be spilt through actions that release or tumble.

The image brought their attention to the carriage of the body in an imaginative way. Their technical execution of the phrase improved as they focused on the image and interpreted it through their actions.

Jackie Mortimer:

This creative approach gave us the opportunity to see students make technical improvements. Exploring through imagery can be a rigorous practice leading to emotional and kinetic understanding. Technique is not simply about physical practice, it has levels of expression. This knowledge is now central to our technical and choreographic work with all students.

Sian Goss:

The students have a better understanding of the compositional process, and this has resulted in improved technique in curriculum work, which can be shared with others visually and verbally.

Ownership

Abi Mortimer:

It is important when considering how to engage young people creatively that you nurture them to take ownership of their roles. The use of imagery is important in generating and understanding movement material as it connects to personal understanding. When creating an environment where students can access imagery and authentic movement, setting tasks is a key skill. This involves giving a thought, idea, image, or stimulus to students and allowing them to explore it for a given time. Although the process is mostly student led the teacher plays a specific role of facilitating an environment where students are motivated and challenged.

Sian Goss:

As teachers we sometimes feed the students too much. It is essential to give younger students the movement vocabulary to work with or it is like trying to write an essay without words. However, it is also vital that you allow students to explore movement vocabulary so they have more ownership. I have adapted tasks from Lîla Dance to suit the students I teach so they could produce movement vocabulary that was their own.

The Mayakaras have become talented choreographers, as is evident in their curriculum work. This has a considerable impact on their peers in lessons. One positive feature is that students share their knowledge, processes and abilities with others, raising the quality of choreographic work. When the class includes a Mayakara, I have seen student attainment improve, as they bring new vocabulary and are confident choreographers. I also feel that the quality of choreographic work in the school is reaching a higher level through the work with Lîla Dance.

Dance teachers are also experimenting with a student led approach to learning and sometimes let go of conventional teaching methods.

The teaching is changing in a number of ways, such as:

- More co-construction between staff and student, with students becoming autonomous in learning but also in the teaching of tasks
- Allowing students more voice in how they develop their work
- Teachers giving students ownership of their material
- More personalised feedback
- The teacher becoming a facilitator
- Students allowed time to experiment and reflect

Abi Mortimer:

Tasks break up the traditional format of the class, as the teacher no longer dictates from the front, and consequently the hierarchy shifts. Task setting gives students the opportunity to make their own discoveries and creates important changes in their learning. Images can be brought into play and the students are able to take ownership over the vocabulary they produce because it comes from them.

Comment from a year 8 Mayakara at the end of the project:

> ... so when Abi and Carrie are asking us to do our own choreography, you've got like that person's idea but then you've got little ideas off of that. So it's still like original, but it's like other people have helped you come up with the idea

Why is it important that students feel they own the material? You could argue that students are engaged if they are copying movement from another body and mimicking it as their own. It is true that to mimic successfully the student must be engaged, but are they engaged creatively? I have found that deep levels of engagement in the creative process only occur when students are in it, own it, live it and feel it. In the best examples of creating movement students do not separate the content from themselves as it does not exist outside their own body. At this level of engagement they are no longer concerned with what is right or wrong, correct or incorrect, as that is no longer relevant. There is a place for right and wrong in dance, but I am talking about engaging students in a creative place where expression and belief are vital. For many young people this can be daunting, and to nurture a deeper level of engagement it is essential to dispel the idea that a response is wrong.

Ownership and engagement
Jackie Mortimer:

We have enjoyed debate about the difference between engagement and creative engagement during the DPC project. Engagement is often what teachers describe as 'on task'. However, creative behaviour does not always conform to on-task codified behaviours. Those students who are creatively engaged seem to challenge, ask more questions, disagree and take risks. We have allowed ourselves to set tasks which develop the individual through emotional, cognitive and physical expression. All students who engage work within the boundaries of the task but those who find creative engagement absorb the task into their bodies. They develop an ownership which allows for creative lines of flight and discover that the task is simply a means but not the end.

Sian Goss:

This is clear when you watch and teach students in lessons. I see evidence of their development through: an improved approach to team work, the ability to make independent decisions, confidence to work alone and in groups in a focused way, and using their initiative. This can daunt students who have not been a Mayakara and diminish their confidence. It is our job to guide The Mayakaras to channel their confidence appropriately without becoming arrogant or domineering, in a way that allows all students to strive towards achieving a high level of work.

Abi Mortimer:

Case study: Sixes
We gave The Mayakaras a task which we call 'sixes'. It is quite functional but is designed to evoke an emotional and meaningful response from the group:

> Two people sit on the floor opposite one another. They are asked to concentrate on one another and bring their focus inward (often the most difficult part of the process!). One dancer picks six places on the other's body and then touches these places in a fixed order. The process is like mapping; it is repetitive and continuous. When this is established, the students vary the quality of touch so that the first might be soft, the second strong, the third a caress and so on. If engaged, the touching becomes meaningful. If they are not already doing so the person being touched is allowed to respond and the body positions and use of space is allowed to shift.

When watching The Mayakaras do this exercise it appeared that some couples were transported outside and beyond the task and onto a unique emotional journey. A literal narrative did not emerge but the couples seemed to experience a variety of sensations that evoked different interpretations. Those couples that did not engage – and not all could – did the task but had little to say about the experience, appearing detached from its creative possibilities.

Feedback
Abi Mortimer:

Feedback is a very important part of the creative process as it opens possibilities for discussion. It provides a springboard for students to encourage deeper responses and explorations.

Regular discussions and feedback are essential to the development of the students' work on movement tasks. Providing specific feedback to the group or individual opens up further discussion, motivating the dancers to question what they have created. Within this feedback we often set mini-tasks – a task within a task. This is always specific to the groups' initial response so that the mini-task is reflexive and can occur as often as the group is willing to respond, but the main aim is to provide challenges.

Jackie Mortimer:

Teachers need to develop an extensive vocabulary and a sense of when to give feedback to bring about a response, as in the example of the glass of water case study. Teachers observed Lîla Dance deliver a balance of repetition with feedback to help students reach a better understanding of technical awareness. If the moment was lost, the student was able to relocate the sensation through returning to the image and reconnecting with it to find the movement and the quality.

Figure 4.2: Students observing their peers which leads to further discussion and peer feedback.

Sian Goss:

Although discussion and reflection are common processes in school, not enough attention is given to them during the feedback process. This is often due to lack of time in short lessons. This process should be embedded, in order to develop the students' analytical skills. Open-ended questions are encouraged and frequently used within the school to foster active participation, and this does help to develop critical abilities.

Abi Mortimer:

Discussion between Lîla Dance and The Mayakaras happens when we review the work as a group. It is informal and provides an opportunity to share, evaluate, analyse and discuss the possibilities for the evolving work. These discussions often begin with open questions such as: 'what does that section say about your partner-ships?'; 'what do you think the audience will think of that situation?'; 'what does it feel like to perform that section?' In these discussions imagery both old and new often comes back, and the meaning behind the movement, emotional, physical or intellectual, comes to the fore. Sometimes these discussions become hands-on, and we may ask the dancers to direct a section of the work to refresh and develop the intention of the movement. The activity is an opportunity for feedback and a pro-cess which develops understanding as the direction is done aloud and in front of the group.

Figure 4.3: Abi, on the left, reviews their work with The Mayakaras as they discuss the evolving choreography

Implications

Abi Mortimer:

People and groups are all different and therefore no one can produce a fail-safe approach to engaging young people in a creative process. This chapter reflects on working practices in a particular situation. We invite you to take a strand from this chapter that is particularly to your liking and use, change, adapt it, to make it useful. The question is not: is it true? but: does it work? What new thoughts does it trigger? What new methods might be inspired? The possibilities and limitations within any given situation are unique. The same task, delivered in the same way, by the same people will have a different outcome when delivered to a different group of young people. What may be extremely successful with one group may be unproductive with another. Because there are always so many variables, a successful activity may not be reproduced with the same group on another day due to the group dynamics or the time of day.

Sian Goss:

This is also true of any school day when the bell signifying the end of a lesson stops students becoming creatively engaged. One student may work better in the morning while another prefers the latter part of the day, but in a tightly structured time-table this cannot be planned. The best choreographic work takes place in double lessons, after school or at weekends, in my experience. The Mayakaras work has allowed us to identify conditions which lead to excellence in learning. Some of these conditions are:

- a bright and colourful classroom environment
- teachers and learners co-inhabiting the space
- shared space and open space
- greeting students at the beginning of the lesson
- a minimum of teacher talk

The wide age range of The Mayakaras makes you question whether our lessons are challenging students. Some teachers have had to let go of preconceptions about young people's ability in dance being determined solely by their age. If the curriculum becomes boring and not challenging enough this can cause problems. This has made me work harder as a teacher, to try and ensure students are being pushed and that I do not limit my expectations.

Abi Mortimer:

I believe the golden rule in any situation is to be reactive to the group and responsive to their achievements. What has grabbed them and why? I recommend you to be brave enough to abandon plans in order to allow deeper exploration of what seems to carry resonance at any particular time. When there is a curriculum to follow this is not easy and the DPC project can produce results which are hard to obtain in the school timetable. It grants the artist time and freedom to respond to the needs of individuals and the group.

However, even in very structured situations the principles can be re-ignited to a smaller or greater extent and made useful where appropriate. As a choreographer for the AQA (Assessment and Qualifications Alliance www.aqa.org.uk) GCSE (General Certificate of Secondary Education) set study, I often teach groups of students with a wide range of abilities. Even when teaching something so specific and precise, I am able to pry open spaces for creative engagement through the use of imagery and task setting. This makes the study relevant and more accessible to the students. What I always find useful is to ask: what are the moments that the students are grabbing? How do I find a way to inject more of this kind of understanding into the whole?

Conclusion

The process of actively seeking to engage students creatively through the use of imagery, ownership and feedback is designed to encourage dancers to locate their artistic ideas and encourage lines of questioning. At the heart of Lîla Dance's work with The Mayakaras is the development of the becoming artist. In all learning experiences the students are presented with avenues and possibilities for further development and exploration. The teaching of a phrase, for example, is opened up through the use of imagery, discussion and task setting, so students learn how to construct a phrase as opposed to imitating the teacher or artist.

The Mayakaras are thinking dancers – movement making is brought to their consciousness and is celebrated at every opportunity. Most importantly, the students learn the means as opposed to the end. They are capable of replicating processes in our absence and applying them to their practice at school.

Jackie Mortimer:

Achieving this level of engagement requires teachers to give students space and time for process as well as time for reflection and discussion. This situation creates an environment where learning becomes co-constructed. It sometimes feels out of control but we have found it to be worth it! Students recognise they have a voice and that their input is valued, and they also give space for others to have opinions. In this situation teachers and students become facilitators, supporting each other.

The concluding comment by Sian, made at the end of the project, reflects on some of the outcomes for students:

Sian Goss:

So this year is very much about their movement and actually that's been the best thing ... it isn't just rep [repertoire] material or set material that they're teaching, it has really pushed them to be creative and them being young artists, and actually that's probably what we want out of the project.

5

Igniting the learning: understanding wisdom of practice

Michael Platt, Kerry Chappell
and Helen Wright

She's a girl that doesn't find school easy ... she's very self conscious ... But I noticed that towards the end of the day she was actually almost playing to the gallery. She was smiling at the visitors, and actually almost trying to catch their eye ... because she wanted, I think, her contribution to be acknowledged. And she was beaming. Well it was really sort of heart warming to see, because here was a girl who's really revelling in what she was doing. And I frankly wouldn't have thought that she'd have made that degree of progress during the course of the day, unless I'd have seen it myself. (Acting Headteacher, Holywells High School, end of project)

Artists and teachers working in performing arts contexts speak of the magical moment when students take ownership of their learning and progress is tangible. The combination of complete immersion, group bonding and embodied connections between the thinking and moving body seems to galvanise participants into a creative flow, which in turn ignites a special energy. These moments happen frequently in lessons, workshops and performances, and the result of one such is captured by this Acting Headteacher. Yet the words to describe and explain how these moments happen remain elusive. We resort to shifting the happening into the realm of the magical, transient and inexplicable.

This research project in the Dance Partners for Creativity (DPC) East of England site, enabled us to examine what makes these hard-to-define magical moments happen. Drawing on approaches in teacher knowledge research (eg Munby, Russell and Martin, 2001) we have attempted to 'find patterned consistency in what is happening in a successful episode of teaching and to find why and how it works' (Leinhardt, 1990:19). To do so we have worked to de-construct the 'wisdom of practice' (Leinhardt, 1990) of the two teacher-artist partner researchers, Michael Platt and Helen Wright. Leinhardt describes wisdom of practice as the 'craft knowledge which encompasses the wealth of teaching information that very experienced practitioners have about their own practice ... a deep sensitive contextualised knowledge' (p18-19). It is this deconstruction process that has enabled us to examine and begin to understand what makes the magical moments happen.

We undertook our DPC research during the fifth year of the project. The practicalities were in place and we had time and space to reflect on the pedagogy which contributes to the evolution of these special moments. Our research team was Michael Platt, Learning and Teaching Advisor for Suffolk Inclusive School Improvement Service, Helen Wright Acting Head of Performing Arts, Holywells High School and Kerry Chappell, DPC Research Fellow.

The project takes place annually in January and involves Year 8 and 9 students (aged 12-13 and 13-14 respectively) from Holywells High School, Key Stage 2 students (7-11 year olds) from two local primary schools and 1st year BTEC (Business and Technical Education Council qualification) Performing Arts students (17 years and over) from Suffolk New College. The project aims to create a vertically grouped learning community whose engagement promotes creativity, collaboration and independence. The final celebration, a shared performance outcome, aims to have an important impact on learning, students' motivation and the development of high quality work. During the 2008 project, Michael ran five half-day workshops with the combined primary and Year 9 students, and Michael and Helen ran five separate half-day workshops with the combined Year 8 and BTEC students. Both project strands came together to share their work at Holywells High School in February with Michael guiding the overall artistic direction.

We worked intensively during the project to collect information about practice and reflected on and analysed it in various ways (see the research text boxes in the chapter).

In the initial planning our roles were clearly defined as either teacher or artist. The integration of these roles was however revealed in the reality of our practice and by the opportunity to analyse our approach. It made most sense to us therefore as a research team to refer to both practitioners involved as teacher-artists. The research highlighted the significance of the dialogue engendered through partnership. Two practitioners bring their wisdom of practice to bear in the same learning context, offering greater potential to extend and challenge learners than if there was only one. This is about not just team teaching but, more significantly, about enabling a shape-shifting relationship between different roles, permitting a simultaneous overview of the learning situation and the detailed focus on individual needs (see also Chapter 7).

Our research and analysis revealed the importance of an openness and flexibility which allowed us to move between roles or to share them as our intuitive wisdom of practice enabled us to respond to the learning context's developing needs. This cycle of doing, reflection and analysis led to a 'deconstruction of the practice in the partnership, in order to rebuild it as the project is happening' (Rolfe, Platt and Jobbins, 2010:106).

Research process: Honing the question

We began by posing ourselves a broad research question. We then gathered and analysed information that helped us refine the question, and finally analysed the information we had to answer that question. Our first question was 'How does the relationship between art and the 'social' in a creative collaborative project, influence the quality of learning?' Our final question was 'What aspects of pedagogical partnership practice make the 'magical moments' happen?'

Planning for learning

Through our reflection and analysis we saw that underlying the magical moments was not only wisdom of practice but also examples of what we call the building blocks of effective teaching. We recognise that these building blocks, integrated with the teacher's subject knowledge and curriculum requirements, are methods of structuring and planning that are commonly used in dance and other disciplines. Identifying them has helped us explore how they contribute to the creation of the magical moments – but they are not the elusive aspects of practice that we wanted to understand. Secure subject knowledge and application of the building blocks alone do not guarantee that students will be engaged, motivated to participate or empowered to take the leap into collaborative creativity. Therefore, we briefly describe the building blocks we identified, before moving on to the less analysed, perhaps more intuitive aspects of practice, which we feel make the magical moments happen.

> **Research process: Gathering information 1:**
> **Conversations and interviews**
> Initially, Kerry guided recorded discussion and reflection. She used the main DPC research question to encourage Michael and Helen to take on the role of partner researchers and ask their own questions. Increasingly they began to take an active role in guiding the site research and these discussions took on the form of the creative learning conversation described in Chapter 2. We audio-recorded these. In order to gather information from the students we found it best to interview those who were particularly interested. In turn, they interviewed their peers following their experience of being interviewees. At times we also interviewed other adults involved in the project. Interviews often included conceptual drawing exercises. This encouraged thinking and speaking and documented experience non-verbally.

Step-by-step creative challenges

Our planning for each session used a step-by-step approach which facilitated progression through a series of smaller, achievable yet challenging tasks. Each activity involved a creative challenge where we asked students: 'how can you … ? can you find a solution to … ? how can you use your imagination and your body to … ?'

We adopted a short time scale for each step. This promoted a sense of urgency and a realisation that we were on a journey where each task was contributing to something bigger. As Helen commented in a reflective conversation after the project, we were 'building on that concept of challenge over the weeks so that things would be getting progressively more difficult for the students and that actually keeps them involved, it's quite an important idea'. This step-by-step approach created anticipation as students waited for their next challenge. This, in turn, promoted engagement and motivation.

Because of its nature, the outcome of each creative task was open-ended. This required us to assess progress and respond immediately with steps which could layer additional challenges to deepen learning. From the outset we planned for unexpected outcomes which was exciting because it triggered new directions or helped clarify where extra input was required.

The importance of a performance outcome to motivate and drive

The performance outcome was a significant catalyst for students' emerging independence. We were always explicit that the project would culminate in a public performance to generate a tangible goal. It provided a real context in which all students would eventually be working independently in front of an audience, without the teacher-artists. Michael observed how this happened significantly in the final session '... the atmosphere of the room changed from a sort of bubbly and rather fragmented excitement ... to increasingly more and more focus ... it crystallised in that final hour of rehearsal'. A Year 8 student observed how the forthcoming performance was promoting a sense of achievement: 'Like really proud of myself because I've never remembered anything in my life'. We noticed that the successes during the step-by-step process had a self-perpetuating effect. The students cumulatively built the positive group ethos as the performance approached.

Cross phase working
The degree of independent thought exhibited by the older students was a significant benefit of the cross phase working and had a powerful impact on the younger students. Initially this manifested itself in the work ethic of all the students. When working on a creative step, the older students exhibited independence which enabled them to continue to develop and refine ideas. This initiative was a powerful role model for the younger students and reinforced our high expectations of student independence. One of the BTEC students observed that in the cross phase working groups: 'They were telling me what to do, which is the way I think it should be ... you should learn from them and they should learn from you'. This suggests that cross phase learning can and does take place irrespective of age or experience.

Teaching for independence and ownership
From the outset, pedagogical practice to facilitate student independence and ownership was fundamental. We knew we could not assume the students would have the experience, maturity or self-confidence to be successful independent learners, so teaching for independence held equal importance to teaching for creativity. In the first session we communicated our belief that an ability to work independently and collaboratively was a key to the success of the project and we subsequently continued to reinforce. We acknowledged and celebrated student progress in working effectively with independence and initiative as much as their creative responses. We also encouraged students to analyse the positive impact of their growing independence on the success of their practice.

We explained that our layers of support as teacher-artists would gradually diminish as we went on a journey towards the performance. This was because we expected the students to develop independent thinking. This quote from Kerry and the Year 8 students acknowledges this:

Kerry: Has he [Michael] been doing anything different, do you think?

Student: Yeah. He's been less in charge.

Kerry: Less in charge? Okay.

Student: Yeah, he's been like, he let us do it. He didn't interrupt like he normally does and he just let us do it.

Research process: Gathering information 2:
Photography, observations and audio diaries
Because of the embodied nature of dance, we wanted to gather information through as many different media as possible. Ultimately we found the combination of photography and observation with written field notes invaluable. Kerry took over 100 photographs in each half-day session that she attended and accompanied these with written field notes. If we were to do further research, we would make photography a higher priority. Michael and Helen also both used audio diaries as a key way to reflect and document their thoughts.

Igniting the learning

The previous section highlights the manner in which a range of elements were planned and implemented during the project. Whilst these contributed to the success of the project, our research has helped us identify the fundamental importance of how the intuitive aspects of our practice (our wisdom of practice) have helped bring them to life and ignite a creative learning culture.

Research process: Analysing information 1:
Collaborative analysis
We shared the analysis of written data and worked to our strengths. We all read our written transcripts from interviews, observations and audio diaries to identify key themes. Then Kerry, the university researcher with more analytic experience, carried out cycles of detailed constant comparative analyses guided by Helen and Michael's input.

Using the lighthouse beam

'I'm like a lighthouse' (Michael, mid-project)

Figure 5.1: Michael, in the background, in 'lighthouse' role, overseeing from the side

In our reflections the teacher-artist role was often referred to as both 'the captain – steering the ship' and 'the lighthouse' which cast its beam across the proceedings. To promote creativity and collaboration we needed to ensure that the student experience was not an adult-led voyage. Of key importance to this was the lighthouse role of observation and listening. This cast a slightly detached, questioning beam across the ongoing work. It heightened our awareness of progress and response, successes and needs. We had questions constantly running through our heads, with Michael asking:

Are they on task?

Are they collaborating?

Is one student dominating?

Are they supporting each other?

Are they concentrating?

Are they interested?

Are they enjoying the work?

The messages received from the lighthouse beam perspective inspired us to respond to what was happening. Michael refers to this as '... part of the creative flow – it takes you somewhere that you weren't anticipating because you can't predict what their response will be artistically or socially'.

The internal dialogue which results from the lighthouse beam can empower the teacher-artist to make creative decisions on how to mould and sculpt the immediately developing lesson ie short term information. It can also give direction to the work's organic long term development.

Short term information on:	**Long term information on:**
☐ Lesson pace	☐ Need to break down ideas further
☐ Student engagement, enjoyment, involvement	☐ If further stimuli are required
☐ Specific student needs and support	☐ Need for more modelling/ support
☐ Success to share and celebrate	☐ Positive responses to be developed
	☐ Unexpected ideas to be embraced to develop work
	☐ New directions stimulated by student response
	☐ Ideas which are not working and should be abandoned/changed

There were always two of us working together in the teacher-artist role and this allowed one of us to take on the more detached role of the lighthouse. We could do this knowing that the other was working in a more hands on capacity with the students. Often the solo teacher has to take on both these roles, which can be challenging, particularly with a mixed ability group, students with behaviour or learning needs or large groups. Our project highlighted the effectiveness of partnership to enable this role-shifting between close up and detached involvement. Michael acknowledged that the slight detachment he experienced in the lighthouse role was possible only because of his confidence and trust in the role Helen was adopting:

the lighthouse ... it feels like I can do that and not feel that I'm sacrificing individuals along the way with the desire to keep the whole moving. Because you're there, if you like, making sure they're coming with us on that journey ...

Immersing in the landscape

As teacher-artists, we were engaged in being reactive translators of our planned building blocks into vibrant, organic, learning situations. Our complete physical and vocal immersion in the immediacy of the landscape of learners contrasted with the detachment of the lighthouse role. This challenged us to apply our full range of physical and vocal qualities to ignite and sustain the learners. Some activities demanded more of this high-energy input than others. It was particularly necessary if the students were reticent about committing to a challenge which pushed them beyond their normal experience. After a session which focused on the development of contrasting qualities of movement, Michael reflected on how he and Helen had drawn on their own resources to encourage student engagement:

> We were at different points in that large space, and so wherever the students were they were getting this almost force field of sound and movement, body percussion, we were using everything we had as teachers to really inspire and motivate the students ... we as the teacher-artist combination were throwing in as much energy and as much direction and as much encouragement and as much praise as possible to really try and inspire and galvanise the group into accessing this dynamic quality and the contrasts that they needed.

We were constantly engaged in a verbal, spatial and physical dialogue, shifting between a number of 'narrator' roles to support, encourage, motivate and challenge the learners.

Questioning narrator

We were creating a soundscore full of questions to accompany and challenge the students whilst they were moving, improvising and performing. We wanted to promote a connection between the moving body and the thinking mind. One series of questions demonstrates this: 'How far can you go? What are your hands doing? Where are you looking? How strong / light can you be?'. In this role we were encouraging thinking dancers who could understand, embody and communicate the intention of their movements.

Praising narrator

Through the lighthouse observation we noted student responses which we wanted to acknowledge with praise because of:

- ◼ originality and creativity
- ◼ participation and commitment
- ◼ collaboration and cooperation

Being able to identify why we recognised a response as significant enabled us to qualify the praise so students could understand what was important. Sometimes this praise was private to an individual or group, as we moved 'intently through the space commenting and encouraging' (Kerry's observation, mid project). Or successes could be celebrated more publicly with the rest of the group.

Dynamic performer/narrator

There were times when we drew on our own skills as performers in a simultaneous fusion of vocal, spatial and physical qualities to engage, motivate and stretch the students:

- ◼ vocally: we invested words with the dynamic quality – pitch – tone – tempo – resonance – appropriate to the movement response
- ◼ spatially: we utilised the impact and effect of shifting spatial proximity to the students
- ◼ physically: we drew on a range of appropriate actions and dynamics to dance with the students, mirroring and extending their responses while modelling high expectations of full embodiment

Figure 5.2 opposite shows Helen doing this in action.

Research process: Analysing the information 2: Flickr and See/Think/Wonder

We created a password protected space online using the photograph website Flickr to store and share selected research photographs. The Flickr commentary tools allowed us to analytically annotate the photographs utilising the See/Think/Wonder protocol from Harvard Project Zero (Tishman and Palmer, 2006). This involves the analyser making increasingly detailed observations of what they see in the photograph, what it makes them think about the situation being photographed and, in turn, what it makes them wonder about the research question under investigation.

Figure 5.2: Helen, crouching, up close with students igniting them as a dynamic performer

Teaching for embodiment

Each of the narrating roles were ways in which we strived for student embodiment of the material and its expression through the dynamics of movement. This was a fundamental component of igniting the learning. When Michael observed this embodiment he commented 'they're dancing with complete conviction, complete understanding of why they are doing it ... They were really taking risks with what they were doing ... It was quite exhilarating to watch'.

Mind and body connection

Having a stimulus for the project and articulating this to the students through a range of supporting material ie words, text, visual image and film, made sure there was a movement intention which was accessible to the student

Figure 5.3: Students immersed mind and body in creating 'The Bridge'

dancers. The lighthouse and narrator roles were opportunities to analyse, promote and strengthen this understanding of intention. Through constant cross-referencing we challenged the students to make connections between the activity they were engaged in and how it related to the stimulus. They were also given frequent opportunities to articulate the intention of what they were doing. We believe it was our emphasis on facilitating student awareness of why they were doing particular movements which led to their ability to connect their movements through mind and body, as shown in Figure 5.3.

Communication – from internal to external

In the performance, the final layer of facilitating embodiment enabled students to develop an awareness of what they were communicating through their movement to an audience and each other. Helen described this process as 'internalising those feelings and then expressing them externally'. This demanded that each student took responsibility for their individual movement contribution to a dance whose intention could be effectively communicated as a whole. Our lighthouse role was a powerful tool in observing this effect. Through the narrator role, we spontaneously articulated and reflected back to the students what impression their movement was making on us, as observers. This allowed them to consider how this was achieved.

Igniting through high expectations

Our knowledge and awareness of a visualised outcome at the beginning was a guiding light, a goal, which we were striving to achieve. This empowered us with single-minded determination.

This clarity promoted our confidence to step back and reflect on progress in an analytic way. Rather than be deflected by a negative student reaction, socially or creatively, it enabled us to reassess how we were working, to change direction, to offer new stimuli and to make the steps smaller or more challenging.

The research enabled us to reflect on how certainty of student success manifested itself in our pedagogy.

Rigorous reinforcement of high expectations

We continually reinforced our high expectations of the students' work ethic, performance quality, collaborative skills and ability to critically assess their own and others work. We did this through the use of language, images, modelling and demonstration.

An example of this was the teacher-led warm up which we developed to incorporate student-led sessions. Planned across five weeks, the significant elements of high quality performance (eg focus, extension, quality of movement) were constantly reinforced within the basic exercises. The language and concepts could therefore be applied with understanding in the performance.

Success was recorded during the project through student voice captured on paper, photos and film. This created a vibrant evidence trail which could be constantly referred to and added to as students' understanding of their ability to be successful grew. Their success creatively, artistically, independently and collaboratively was recorded (see also Research process boxes: Gathering information 1 and 2).

Realistic time scales

Successful outcomes take time to be achieved. They require foundations of experience on which students can build their practice confidently. This perception of success as progression towards a goal helped us break the work down and not expect too much too soon. We could thus gauge an outcome successful for the stage the students were at. In turn this informed us of the direction and level of challenge required to move them on to the envisaged successful outcome. An example of this was the structured spatial improvisation exercise which was introduced in week one. The students found it very challenging in its freedom of choice. Each week we inserted more challenging activities into the improvisational structure as the students' familiarity with the concept and how they could be successful grew.

Our research revealed the importance of demanding success not only at the end of the project. We were carefully, subtly and overtly constructing the pathways to success through sustained practice from the outset. This led to the kind of achievements recognised by the school's Acting Headteacher:

> ... it's that self confidence to think 'I can do this' ... And I don't think many of them would have said initially that they were capable of reaching those standards, which I thought frankly were very, very impressive.

Research process: Sharing our ideas

By the time we came to pull our ideas together in order to disseminate what we had learned, Helen had resigned her teaching post to go travelling overseas. Through a combination of face to face meetings, email and Facebook postings to Helen, for instance, in Guatemala, we shaped our final analyses into this chapter. Our understanding of what we have learned also exists for all of us in our ongoing embodied practices.

Conclusion

This research project has enabled Michael and Helen, as practitioner researchers, to deconstruct our intuitive practice and identify key elements of our planning methods. We have identified significant areas which contributed to engagement, progression in learning and high quality outcomes. On reflection we have divided these areas into two separate yet interrelated categories: those which enable us to effectively plan for learning and those which ignite the learning. Our research has highlighted the importance of both these components being present in equal measure. For Helen and Michael these findings have been significant in different ways.

Helen left the UK towards the end of the research project to travel around South and Central America for a year. The research findings resonated in her new situation as she witnessed the need to ignite learning, as individuals struggled with the decision to remain at school or provide immediate financial support for their families. She was also struck, however, by the way in which the expressive arts are integral to national culture and identity and are embraced by all. There is not the same need to generate awareness and appreciation of this as there is in the UK. Perhaps, even with all our resources, we can learn something from volunteer projects with little funding who use only what is available: ie a concept of learning through creative play governed by imagination. Now returned and working as a Family Intervention Project Officer, Helen combines the step-by-step approach with her intuition to unravel complex situations. This allows her to offer achievable yet ever-changing and challenging goals that can result in families owning the outcome.

For Michael, who has remained in the UK education system, the research holds different significance: the current emphasis in UK teacher training, professional development and inspection lies predominantly in lesson structures which we have categorised within Planning for Learning. Alongside subject knowledge, these components contribute to ensuring that learning progresses through support and scaffolding but they do not in themselves guarantee creative learning. The intuitive elements of teaching, which we have categorised in Igniting the Learning, contribute to the wisdom of practice. This wisdom is fundamental in realising the planning and making creative learning come alive. It is clear that each practitioner will have their own profile of intuitive preferences which have evolved through their wisdom of practice.

This research is relevant because it identifies the interrelatedness of teaching's structural and intuitive elements. It goes on to suggest that there is a need to counteract the prevailing emphasis on summative assessment with methods which ignite and sustain learning. The dichotomy is similar for learners too: their progress and attainment is identified and driven by National Curriculum Levels often at the expense of opportunities for creative learning. This happens because teachers rely less on the wisdom of their intuitive practice and are constrained by the structural rigour advocated to ensure students pass to the next level.

The numerous guidelines designed to advise and support teachers with the structural elements of teaching acknowledge the need for continuing professional development. This is not the case for the realm of intuitive wisdom, probably because it has not been so rigorously identified. This suggests that teachers might acquire it during their practice by a natural process of osmosis.

The Assessment for Learning training materials (http://nationalstrategies. standards.dcsf.gov.uk/node/97905) highlight the importance of formative assessment. They identify where students are, where they need to get to and what steps are needed to help them get there. This is seen as a prerequisite of effective teaching. Although highlighting individual children's needs, it places pressure on teachers to ensure progression, without necessarily advising them how this can be achieved beyond target setting. This research has contributed to the identification of significant aspects of intuitive practice which facilitate effective formative assessment procedures eg the role of the lighthouse and the narrator. These practices place the individual and the collective at the centre of the learning process. This enables us to respond to the idea that one model doesn't fit all.

We have examined how teacher-artists work in a variety of ways to enable the next steps in learning to happen. But there is still a need to draw on the wider expertise of a range of practitioners to uncover, articulate and celebrate the multiple ways in which intuitive practices are applied to generate outstanding creative learning. This in turn will help build up an explicit body of knowledge equal to that which dominates structural planning for learning. There must be rigour in how this is done so as to forestall the suggestion that this intangible aspect of our practice is in any way secondary or ephemeral. A balance of advice would highlight the validity that there are two interrelated, equal strands of effective teaching for creativity. This would provide a basis for developing the essential pedagogical practice of teachers to support them in making their structural planning translate into effective practice which ignites creative learning.

6

Conversations on the role of play in creative learning environments

Helen Angove and Rachelle Green
with Kerry Chappell

In classrooms that nurture creativity, teachers make spaces for playfulness, helping children incorporate the flexibility and adaptability that is so crucial to creating novel thought. These spaces are embedded within the structure of the class, the schedule of the day and the philosophies of the teachers across a range of curricular areas. And they build on children's natural strengths and abilities. (Shagoury-Hubbard, 1996:130)

Introduction

This chapter is a dialogue between two partner researchers in the South-West Dance Partners for Creativity (DPC) site. We reflect upon our experience of Step Change, a two year Community Dance for Health project run between 2008 and 2010 by Take Art, an arts development agency in Somerset. Rachelle Green was then Deputy Director of Dance and Project Manager of *Step Change* and Helen Angove was one of its dance artists and a peer mentor. Between September 2008 and March 2010, a team of twelve dance artists from Take Art worked with over 60 dance groups in around 35 locations across Somerset. The project was conceived as part of a national drive to create healthier and more active communities by enabling people to take greater control of their lifestyle choices. Participants were grouped into strands: ages 5-14; 14-19; 20-50; 50+ including the frail elderly; and people with learning and physical disabilities. The project was supported by a range of partners from the arts and health sectors and reached over 1,900 people.

This DPC enquiry operated differently from the other partner researcher sites in that it was embedded within the broader remit of *Step Change*. Whilst the core DPC research focused on work with 11-14 year olds and was primarily situated in schools, our work with *Step Change* spanned the ages of 5 to 90. In every learning setting, we advocated the creation of an environment which enabled participants to play, create and learn.

Helen Angove began developing the DPC initiative in the first year of *Step Change* and her reflections relate particularly to the schools strand. In the second year, Rachelle Green assumed responsibility for the continuing enquiry and began to draw greater links between the work Helen had undertaken in schools and its relationship to work in the other four strands. During *Step Change* and since, we continued to work in other sectors but also came together in regular intensive bursts to reflect upon the DPC enquiry. Our diverse experiences and our particular working processes strongly inform our reflections.

In this chapter we review examples of work drawn from *Step Change* and whilst we do not claim to provide definitive answers to our initial research question, we hope to provide fellow practitioners with a possible starting point from which to review their own practice.

The Research Question

We initially wanted to query to what extent notions of play could be used by both teachers and artists as a tool for facilitating creative learning with a particular focus on the Key Stage 3 dance curriculum. When employing the terms 'play' and 'creativity' we recognise that we are drawing upon concepts that are defined and employed in numerous ways, according to context, practice and theoretical perspective. We were locating play as an attitude and a process rather than an activity (Prentice, in Moyles, 1994).

Shagoury-Hubbard (1996) defines playing as 'taking unbridled delight in the doing, immersing ourselves in joyful expression in the here and now; allowing our minds to take flight, imagining and testing out possibilities' (p67). Translated into an educational setting, this relates to the participant's capacity to explore and improvise during their dance lessons and this relies upon the teacher's ability to facilitate play in the form of exploration and improvisation when planning and delivering a session. This requires the teacher to be playful and to think playfully in order to devise innovative activities, delivery modes and structures.

Our literature review revealed a range of factors which regularly appear as the key conditions for creativity and learning in the arts, through different combinations. Between the terms 'play', 'creativity' and 'learning' connections are often assumed or implied. For example, dancers, educators or child psychologists might use these terms in various contexts with different intent. For dance practitioners, the process by which participants learn is as important as what they learn. Thus for us, a creative learning experience would require the participant to explore and improvise so they can engage with and test existing knowledge, develop and refine skills and discover or construct new meanings.

Prentice (in Moyles, 1994) outlines a need for the educator to 'maximise opportunities for creative behaviour' (p130) yet notes that in reality, the necessary conditions can be missing. Therefore the quest to play and be playful was central to our enquiry. The importance of play in children's development as learners is widely documented (Vygotsky, 1978; Bruce, 1991; Bennett, Wood and Rogers, 1997). Shagoury-Hubbard (1996) argues that play requires children to 'grapple with problems, take risks in their thinking, engage in complex and creative problem solving ...' (p68). Thus participation in a playful, creative dance experience would equip learners with knowledge, skills and strategies which might enable them to learn creatively in and from other situations.

We used the initial research question as a starting point from which to reflect upon multiple teaching situations. Here, we each offer our own perspective, shaped by our diverse experiences of working in the fields of secondary, further and higher education, community dance and home education.

Time, space and relationship

> Verbal encouragement of risk-taking, a flexible use of ideas, materials, space and time, must be accompanied by practitioner's personal behaviour which embodies these qualities and classroom organisation which allows such behaviour to flourish. (Prentice in Moyles, 1994:130)

Having observed and facilitated a variety of dance activities over the two year period, we recognised that play was essential for the session to provide a creative learning experience. Three key factors were intrinsically linked to play: space, time and relationship – but these terms have dance specific meanings as well as more general meanings. For example, space might be a literal space (a studio) or a metaphorical space (a particular frame of mind). Time might refer to the duration of a single activity, or an extended learning period of some weeks. Relationship might refer to informal interactions between individuals or to the formal exchanges that take place between teachers, artists and pupils as they perform particular roles within and outside the classroom. The three factors are interdependent and one influences another.

Space, time and relationship are constantly employed within any learning experience, successful or otherwise, and the management or mismanagement of one or more factors can facilitate or inhibit play and playfulness. Accordingly, we use these factors in two ways: as a lens through which to read and interpret a range of specific dance examples and also as tools which might be used to facilitate play and playfulness in the planning, delivery and evaluation of future creative learning experiences.

Observations through the lens

Discussions with dance teachers and practitioners involved in community dance practice and other DPC research sites reveal that we all recognise the pressures imposed by the National Curriculum and acknowledge the risk that our teaching might sometimes be driven by the requirements of syllabi, assessment and quality assurance procedures. More specifically, we agreed that these factors impacted on time, space and relationship and consequently play can lose out. However, we agreed that it should be possible to identify ways in which teachers and practitioners could use play in the three stages of the learning experience – planning, delivery and evaluation – to facilitate a creative learning experience for any participant.

Helen: Logistics play a significant role in relation to time and space in dance sessions. Group sizes tend to be relatively large. There are regularly 25-30 students. Timetabled sessions in schools may only allow 40-50 minutes of dance activity. Often pupils have to move to an alternative space, travel to and from the class and change into suitable clothing before and after lessons. At Key Stage 3, dance is often timetabled in a carousel with other arts subjects or Physical Education. So learners may only study dance for a short period of time, eg one lesson a week for four to eight weeks. It can be tempting to employ a tutor-led teaching model to manage the demands imposed by time, space and curriculum objectives. This guides learners towards pre-planned lesson outcomes and allows little room for experimentation. This might involve learners being closely managed a) spatially, using lines, rows and facing the front; b) temporally, being hurried in and out of lessons, given little time to produce material or for reflection; and c) verbally, being spoken to, told and instructed.

Such methods can be successful in that the lesson aims and learning outcomes are met. Many pupils acquire knowledge and skill when taught in this way. However we query whether lessons of this kind promote learning as a skill in itself. There is little opportunity for learners to develop an autonomous voice or explore their own ideas. So we turned our attention to sessions we had observed in which the teacher or dance artist found creative ways of managing time, space and relationship to create productive learning environments.

Rachelle: I found groups would often work together in a circle. This provided an equal space for participants to share their ideas and a focus for individual learning to occur. All the participants could be seen within this structure, so the movement activities provided a number of spatial scenarios. Some of the groups chose to explore the space in various ways which demonstrated their confidence and trust to improvise within this structure. This model created an inclusive learning environment where everyone could share their ideas and explore their own movement potential.

When looking through the lens of time, the length of the lesson and the length and depth of the project was important to the development of play. Some of the best practice I witnessed illustrated 'that movement activities have been kept similar but have been explored in a variety of ways, intuitively led by practitioners who have the time and space to give insightful feedback to the participants' (observation reports from Step Change: Dance and Health Project 2008-2010).

In the weekly sessions I observed, I became interested in the learning that occurs when dance is not happening. I considered what creative synergies and developments occur for people out of the learning environment. This made me query how a creative learning environment develops ripples of creative thinking in other areas of people's lives. This led me to ask the following questions: How does time impact on learning when sessions are taught weekly for just six weeks or in a consolidated block of time? What learning experience can practitioners facilitate during six weekly 45 minute sessions? How can we play with the curriculum and be creative and innovative with what we deliver?

Helen: A complex set of issues emerged in terms of role and relationship. In sessions where I taught or observed young people in schools, I wondered what impact we, the adults, were having on their learning experience. I suspected that on occasions our presence and performed personas impeded play and creativity. Often the learners' voices seemed strangely silent. Were we preventing the pupils from having a collective or individual voice in their learning? The issue did not seem as simple as an adult-child divide based on age. In contrast, when I worked in youth settings, the relationship with the learners was often far more spontaneous, mutually negotiated and collaborative. So I surmised that the relationship issues came specifically from the teacher-pupil interaction and concerned the performance of defined hierarchical roles. I realised that many of the dance teachers observed, including myself, subtly established and reinforced their role during sessions, often inadvertently, through certain behaviour. For example, teachers often asked pupils to sit down during a practical session whenever they stood and talked. Whilst this might have been done for logistical reasons, out of habit, or because it was a school protocol, it suppressed pupils physically in terms of space and disrupted the flow of their work in terms of time. It also established the teacher as an authority figure who had control of the learning in relation to the students. I became aware of other hierarchical behaviour that I unwittingly used when I was teaching in schools. For example, teachers often tested pupil knowledge through whole class teacher-directed question and answer sessions rather than in free discussion between pupil-pupil and pupil-teacher. Pupils generally had to seek permission to speak by raising their hand. Pupils had little opportunity to negotiate the content, parameters or outcomes of tasks. These forms of behaviour become the norm in schools and may be performed by both teachers and pupils as second nature, thus maintaining the status quo.

Rachelle: Through our observations we agreed that being able to play with ideas, whether as student or teacher, opens the mind and allows boundaries to be transgressed or at least prodded. We discussed whether we were actually working when we play. Was there a meaningful goal? We thought there was. This goal was set by the individual and solutions were personally explored and played with to achieve learning needs.

So what does play facilitate in terms of learning? From my work and reflections, I believe it tests the ability to apply learning, demonstrate understanding and develop creativity. When the creative part of a dance session begins, a real shift happens. There is a lot more discussion, negotiation, problem solving and team work which can unlock individual potential. I observed how the creative dance experience was the catalyst to improved confidence, self-esteem and group cohesion, as well as the physical and emotional health benefits dance activity affords.

Regarding relationships within the creative learning environment, the individual must want to learn and their interest in the world needs to be ignited and nurtured by the teacher. This provides a feeding ground for new ideas to develop and grow. The teacher's role is to ask questions, inspire and stimulate interest and to develop enquiry and interest.

Helen: Rachelle is privileging the autonomy of the learner. She emphasises a need for teaching and learning relationships which foster independent enquiry as well as teaching how to do or what to know. In the different educational settings I have worked in, I realise that the skills and strategies required of children by the Early Years Foundation Stage are completely in tune with this.[1] Learning takes place through creative engagement with resources and play is seen as central to the discovery of knowledge and development of skills.

In contrast, from my work in Higher Education, I know that dance lecturers and practitioners often spend the first year trying to release new students from the rules, regulations and frameworks that have driven their dance work up to that point. First year undergraduates often struggle to argue for and sustain a creative vision which stems from a genuine playful curiosity about ideas and concepts. They have to rediscover improvisational working methods which are not necessarily target driven or product based. They also have to learn that activities might stutter, fail, or receive adverse reactions and employ playful and innovative problem solving skills to devise solutions.

There is a strong argument for re-thinking the rules, regulations and frameworks used when teaching dance in schools in order to provide learners with the necessary dance skills to study dance in Higher Education. This might forge greater links with how dance is delivered in a vocational setting as opposed to a mainstream educational setting. This might in turn mean a focus on specialist pedagogical processes that have been developed by dance artists and practitioners, as opposed to more generic processes employed across secondary education.

Rachelle: I think many of the issues Helen raises at HE level take root at an early stage in children's learning processes because of the values, structures and habits instilled by formal educational contexts in the UK. I see successful creative learning experiences when I watch my own children at play. They negotiate the concepts of time, space and relationship constantly. As a facilitator of young children and as a home educator, I believe maximising learning is about knowing when to direct and structure play, when to add additional stimulus and when to allow free-flow play to evolve.

I have learnt that play requires children to organise personas, roles and relationships and to develop and foster negotiation skills. They learn to compromise and develop intuition through play. This provides them with different ways of looking at the world. And, as Wendell Holmes has said: 'one's mind, once stretched by a new idea, never regains its original dimensions' (cited by James in Dowty, 2000:158).

Ways forward – planning

Helen: In our reflections we identified that play needs to be anticipated and built into planning if it is to occur as a genuine component of school dance sessions. The planning period provides an ideal opportunity to revise how the norms of time, space and relationship are established and how they might be alternatively employed. For example, I have drawn on our DPC reflections and my own planning of creative learning curricula to consider the pros and cons of different modular structures. The following diagrams provide a spatial illustration of different ways in which this might work.

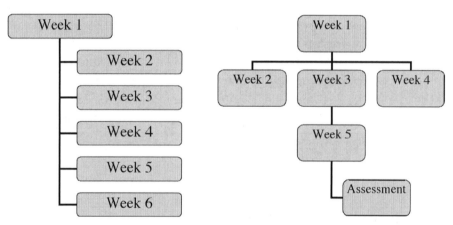

Figure 6.1: Linear, cumulative model of learning

Figure 6.2: Non-linear, progressive model of learning

Figure 6.1 provides a model in which all the key concepts are introduced in the first week. This provides the students with an overview. In the subsequent weeks, individual aspects are explored in a cumulative manner. Students play with each key concept in more depth and this allows layers of knowledge to build up.

Figure 6.2 provides a model in which, like figure 6.1, the ideas are all introduced in week 1. In weeks 2 to 4, specific concepts are explored in more depth. The model is progressive but it is not linear and weeks 2 to 4 can occur

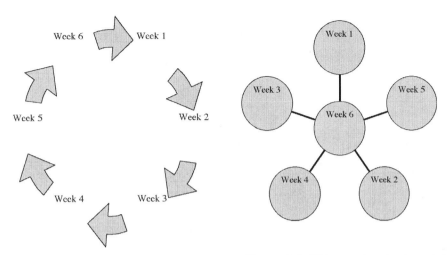

Figure 6.3: Cyclical model of learning   Figure 6.4: Rhizome-inspired model
of learning

in any order. This would allow the teacher to play more freely with the lesson content by responding to the outcomes of previous lessons. Moreover week 5 inter-relates the ideas studied in weeks 1 to 4. This might allow individual students to present different ideas, outcomes and solutions to those previously developed.

Figure 6.3 shows another progressive model. This one uses a cyclical structure in which each week leads to the next in a cumulative manner like figure 6.1. However unlike figure 6.1, this model emphasises repetition and deepening of learning as the cycle of six weeks is continually repeated. This would ideally allow for new information to be introduced as the cycle begins again whilst original material is re-visited. Play could operate as a problem-solving strategy, a means by which to review and rework ideas.

Figures 6.4-6.6 employ non-linear approaches to learning. In figure 6.4, a rhizome-based model is shown. The final week 6 sits at the centre of the learning experience. Weeks 1 to 5 all lead to week 6, but can be taught in any order as they do not link to each other in a progressive manner. This system

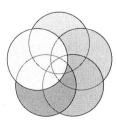

Figure 6.5: Holistic model of learning

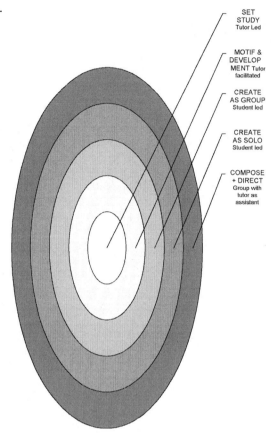

Figure 6.6: From tutor-led to autonomous model of learning

SET STUDY Tutor Led

MOTIF & DEVELOPMENT Tutor facilitated

CREATE AS GROUP Student led

CREATE AS SOLO Student led

COMPOSE + DIRECT Group with tutor as assistant

would allow the teacher to move through the scheme of work in a responsive and playful way. The teacher could find a relevant order as the weeks progressed, rather than following a pre-determined journey.

Figure 6.5 is a useful model for teachers who want to deliver the curriculum in a holistic manner. It would allow them to continually illustrate and explore relationships between ideas or themes or compositional elements. This model would also enable the practitioner to play with the curriculum in both the planning and delivery stages.

Figure 6.6 is the model that deals most specifically with relationships as the teacher role changes from week to week. This shifts the pupils towards autonomous learning. In my experience this model has certainly facilitated an increased use of play by the learners.

Ways forward – delivery

Rachelle: The lens of time, space and relationship enables us continually to revise, to play and vary the ways in which learning occurs. Through our investigations we have found play to be the foundation for creative learning. So how can we as teachers start to play?

How can we use the space we teach in innovatively? How can we make use of resources and manage the obstacles where we work? How can outside space provide an additional resource when we consider play? Can we think about the impact of spatial orientation eg the tutor pupil divide; the impact of levels eg pupils sitting and teachers standing; and the impact of directions eg lines facing the front? Can we reflect on how spatial decisions communicate information about status and role?

How, as teachers, can we play with time in our sessions? Can we strive for depth of learning rather than breadth of information delivered? How might this be achieved within our individual school settings?

How can we facilitate autonomous learning outside the classroom? Can we use preparatory or follow up tasks for students? Doing so would enable pupils to learn at their own pace, consolidate knowledge and apply ideas introduced in the classroom. In turn this would demonstrate their individual understanding and allow the teacher to check that learning has taken place.

In terms of relationships, to truly facilitate a playful, creative learning experience, the teacher/practitioner needs to find ways of subverting hierarchical frameworks. These can influence our teaching, and it is vital that we create an environment in which the learner becomes a co-collaborator. This requires a significant shift in the roles of both learner and teacher. For example: the teacher might revise their role as teacher and encourage the student voice to be heard more. This would also enable pupils to learn how to learn as well as learning how to dance, and thus gain skills in, for example, problem solving, negotiation and time management.

The teacher might also invite the learners to negotiate and construct a set of expectations for the dance lessons. These could acknowledge how different roles and relationships could be inhabited within the confines of that particular session. This would enable the pupils to acknowledge that different relationships are acceptable in different contexts, as long as boundaries are jointly agreed and not transgressed.

Conclusion

In this chapter we have begun to consider some of the factors that inform and shape creative learning environments. Due to the parameters of our enquiry and its constrained time and resources, we have not provided a definitive model for creative learning, nor have we proposed fail-safe solutions to the problems we have raised. Nonetheless we hope that our reflections will provide a framework for fellow teachers, practitioners and artists to build upon.

Helen: We have used evaluation to review a range of examples and make suggestions regarding planning and delivery. However, I would like to conclude by considering the value of play as a critical and evaluative tool which operates beyond its immediate application to practitioners' planning and delivery. Play can facilitate in depth engagement with, and analysis of, the traditions and norms inherent in the regulatory structures that underpin mainstream education. I would therefore like to propose additional ways in which we can open up reflective debate about the value of play and its impact on the facilitation of learning in mainstream education. In particular, I am interested in the notion of 'serious play' (Freud, 1908) as an evaluative tool. Freud suggests that 'a child creates a world of his own, or, rather, re-arranges the things of his world in a new way' (Freud, 1908:132). Like the child in Freud's quote, a practitioner, teacher or curriculum manager could engage in 'serious play' in order to review, re-conceptualise and re-create the immediate teaching and learning situation as well as the frameworks that shape, inform and restrict it.

Rachelle: For us, playing is about giving time and space to trying out different ideas which might culminate in interesting solutions. It is about the individual taking responsibility for their learning. This can happen for people in various ways at different stages of their lives. The challenge is working with people to find the unique combination of time, space and relationship that facilitates their learning. Ultimately it is for us to play with these concepts as facilitators to enable participants to engage in a creative learning experience.

Note

1 Further information about the Early Years Foundation Stage (EYFS) can be found at http://nationalstrategies.standards.dcsf.gov.uk/earlyyears

PART THREE
CREATIVITY AND PARTNERSHIP –
BUT WHAT KINDS?

Figures 7.1-7.3: Sarah's bridge crossing

7

Journeys of becoming: humanising creativity

Kerry Chappell

I watched as Sarah nervously took hold of the long sticks. Her attempts to hide behind her fringe seemed futile but she kept trying. I imagined her thinking 'why me? It's too scary ... I might fall off'. I was beginning to wonder myself why they'd asked the students to do this. They'd given them a few props – long sticks and big old bent carpet sample books – and asked them to work in groups of about ten to make a bridge for one student to get across the room without touching the floor. The idea came from a character's journey in the Indian myth they were working on. Helen was part of Sarah's group and was nudging them along with their ideas, but some of the students said they were nervous about hurting or embarrassing themselves, although a couple had also said it would be pretty amazing if it worked. Helen and Michael had already stretched them quite a long way that day by asking Siobhan, one of the Year 8s, to lead the warm up for all the students. This included a group from the local college who were a couple of years older. At the time I'd wondered if she'd pull it off, but after a false start when one of her friends had to remind her of the sequence, she'd done OK.

With the help of Elsa and Aarti, Sarah pushed herself up and stepped onto the bridge of hands. Michael had asked them to make the journey slow and careful, with the student who was crossing the bridge looking out into the distance, so Sarah couldn't just hurl herself along. With Elsa and Aarti taking her weight with the long sticks, Sarah started to make her way over the interlocked hands, flicking her fringe out of her eyes as she went. After trying out various ideas from different people, the group had decided that once Sarah had passed each pair they should run to the front to extend the bridge. This meant that they had to sprint down the side of the line otherwise Sarah would step onto nothing. When she had nearly reached the other side of the room, the hands underneath her weren't locked properly and her footing started to slip. I was sitting very close by and lurched forward to grab an arm but Cara, who was right next to Sarah, managed to get underneath her and, with Helen's help, caught her as she came down. Sarah looked utterly relieved. She looked up and realised that she'd made it to the other side. As she slid back behind her fringe, the smile on her face said it all. (Collated fieldnotes East of England site, end of project)

Why was this journey in this site so significant? What kind of creativity is threaded through this experience (Figures 7.1-7.3) and others like it within DPC?

Across the Dance Partners for Creativity (DPC) research, I have been able to enquire into and analyse scenarios like the one described and to explore them in relation to data and reflections from other DPC university and partner researchers. It has given me the chance to try to understand these journeys taking place within secondary school dance education, and to draw also on previous theorising within dance education and wider education to build on the idea of creativity as humanising. In working to understand why journeys like Sarah's are important in terms of the kind of creativity that they illustrate, this strand of DPC offers insight into people's 'becoming' and the journeys this entails.

What kinds of creativity and partnership?

This question of the kind of creativity became critical to the DPC team because we were all involved in different capacities in facilitating creativity in educational partnerships. We all found ourselves responding to requests to 'provide' creativity in schools. What did we each mean by 'creativity'?

For the DPC university researchers located within the Exeter University CREATE Research Group (Chappell, 2008; Rolfe *et al*, 2009; Craft *et al*, 2008) creativity broadly speaking is positioned as ubiquitous and playful and exists within an ethical framework. In relation to Banaji, Burn and Buckingham's (2010) rhetorics, it also has political and democratic dimensions.

However, our position sits in tension with three other discourses connected to creativity as discussed in Chapter 1 but I briefly repeat them here. Firstly, our approach counters the idea of creativity as individualised, marketised, globalised and universalisable. Secondly, DPC challenges the educational performativity agenda's narrowing focus on achievement in core learning areas. It aims to avoid harnessing creativity to performativity but instead values creativity in its own right. Thirdly, our approach to creativity sits within a discourse which sees young people as capable, active and empowered rather than as passive, vulnerable and in need of protection (Craft, 2011).

In order to challenge these discourses through empirical research, we have focused on humanising creativity, developed from my study of creativity in primary level dance education (Chappell, 2008).

Humanising creativity positions it as individual, collaborative and communal. Communality is key to the humanising process. It encourages empathy, shared ownership and the understanding that creativity is an emotional journey and not always fun. It often requires creators to engage with communities and cultures which have other values and so involves conflict and difference. It is a process of change which is mindful of its consequences, a process of becoming (Chappell, 2008).

Humanising creativity is firmly positioned as an antonym to the three discourses above but it resonates with the discourse of democratic and political creativity. Accepting and negotiating conflict is part of the humanising creative process. So is the idea of not burying difficulty and difference, allowing voices to be heard that might not usually be given space, and for those voices to influence change. Humanising creativity also resonates with aspects of the discourse of creativity as social good, as it puts the values of school and wider community to the fore of communal activity. It has much in common with Craft *et al*'s (2008) argument for educators to take responsibility for a wise dimension to creativity. The DPC analysis has highlighted the potentially humanising role of creativity and provided an opportunity to develop it further.

DPC is about exploring the nature and development of co-participative partnership, as well as acknowledging difference. We understand the complexity of interaction and negotiation in light of Jeffery's (2005) research, investigating dialogic engagement in partnerships, and take it as a starting point.

Research process
As described in Chapter 2, the university team led on the over-arching research question: what kinds of creative partnerships are manifested between dance-artists and teachers in co-developing the creativity of 11-14 year olds? I have looked at two layers within this question: firstly what kinds of creative partnerships were manifested and secondly the kind of creativity that ensued.

Importantly, we have sought to create a research space which is underpinned by a socially constructed view of reality and influenced by critical theory, and which allows for multiple, possibly different perspectives which promote change. I am not writing on behalf of the external and school partners; I offer another rigorous perspective on the data, informed by my previous research and experience. I aim to demonstrate something of the unique contribution that dance has to make to creativity in education.

Journeys of becoming
Partnerships of multiple shifting identities

Returning to Sarah's bridge-crossing and similar journeys within DPC sites, four key intertwined partnership characteristics laid the ground for humanising creativity and its process of becoming. These characteristics can be seen as the partnership framework for Part 3, underpinning the discussions of partnership in Chapters 8 and 9.

Students as partners

We assumed that we were exploring partnerships between school and external partners but found partnerships between school and external partners and also students. In the South-East site Abi, one of the external partners described the relationship as a 'two way street ... we still learn from them ... it's not about hierarchy'. There the teachers took a supporting role to the artist-student relationship. This was less apparent in the other sites, but hierarchies were always to some degree flattened so the students were seen as genuine partners. For example Helen, the school partner, was a creative collaborator with the students in the example introducing this chapter.

Multiple identity shifting

The site partnerships were characterised by participants engaging in multiple identity shifting between identities such as: teacher, performer, maker, choreographer, surrogate family member, facilitator, artist, learner, manager, rehearsal director. Shifting was often spatial and embodied and it could be problematic. For example, Siobhan, as shown in this chapter's opening, was carefully helped into taking the identity of teacher. The spatiality and embodiment of this was key to standing in front of the group in a large gymnasium, and physically engaging more than thirty people.

The data records examples of students, school and external partners in all the roles above, and it was important that identity-shifting was appropriate. Certain people took on some roles more than others and not everyone took on every role. Students and staff were facilitated to let go of their normal identities and step into new ones, however difficult this might be, particularly for the younger students. Midway through their research, Bim and Caroline, the London site partners, remarked 'that's what's brilliant, we're both having to let go'. Both were aware that this required significant honesty and trust.

Multiple leadership positioning

People also positioned themselves in relation to each other in different leadership identities. These, too, were spatially manifested in an embodied way. The four types of leadership position students, external partners and/or school partners took on were: leader, co-leader, inclusive leader and no leader. Leader entailed one person guiding progress; co-leading meant two or more individuals collaboratively guiding activity. An inclusive leader adopted a flattened hierarchy which incorporated different voices within a small group. For example in the East of England site Adrian, an older college student, created ideas with two year 8 students, guiding development which included everyone's ideas. No leader meant that no-one was identified as leading; leadership was present but dispersed, as often happened around performances. As one East of England student commented before the performance: 'I don't think anybody's leading now. I think we're all working together'.

Shared creative group identity

In all three sites, a shared creative group identity provided a safe place to create. These identities were artistic. Abi, a South-East England external partner, described her connection with the student group as 'fundamentally artistic'. Relationships within the artistic group were often referred to in family terms: Helen, the East of England school partner, described herself as 'a mother hen ... a surrogate parent ... more than just teacher/pupil, [a] different sort of relationship'. Shared group identity as a creating community required considerable empathy. Helen stated: 'The students developed their own sense of support for one another to support Siobhan creatively. When she's leading, there's this, yes, sense that they don't want her to fail and so they're helping her out'. Social relationships acted through mindful responsibility, gluing together the partnerships' identity and creative work.

Positioning and sharing identity

Why then are these particular characteristics pivotal to the creativity of students like Sarah? Moje and Luke (2009) offer a helpful strand of identity theorising, arguing for identity as socially constructed, fluid, multiple and in process. In my field notes above, we see identity enacted in this way. DPC identity-shifting and leadership positioning resonate with what Moje and Luke (2009) call the metaphor of 'identity as position'. Rooted in the theories of Foucault and Bourdieu, this discourse demonstrates that power relations shape identities by calling on people to occupy a particular position (or not).

In the evidence we see everyone invited to step into new, unusual identities. Moje and Luke argue that 'as people experience certain positions ... they come to imagine future positions and their future selves moving within and across these positions' (p431). They suggest that identities can be quilted, with multiple identities existing in parallel and enacted at different times. Thus identity is fragmented and in tension; and this reflects the DPC findings that while identities shifted this could be a problematic process.

Students became accustomed to going beyond the everyday way that they were expected to construct their identities spatially. This liberated them to imagine new future social positions and identities for themselves and thus empowered them to create new ideas and possibilities. It opened the space for Siobhan to imagine and enact leading the warm up and for Sarah to become the person who crossed the bridge and embodied her group's new idea.

Moran and John-Steiner (2004) emphasise the importance to successful creative collaboration of developing a shared group identity or 'figured world'. These worlds were a temporary aspect of DPC projects and they provided a communal, safe, artistic space within which participants like Sarah could have and *become* exciting creative ideas.

Collaborative physical generation: stretching inside-out and outside-in
With these partnership characteristics structuring activity, we turn to the creativity. Crucial to students having and becoming new creative ideas was the interaction of individual, collaborative and communal physical generation where people created from inside themselves to the outside and outside themselves to the inside. This is a theme from previous research (Chappell, 2006) which appears here strongly but with more complexity. Participants were able to bring themselves and their ideas into conversation with other people, other people's ideas, and the developing artistic idea.

The students in Sarah's group discussed how working together on the bridge task, which they viewed as 'high risk', led to exciting collaborative creativity:

Chris: It opens doors

Ella: ... [you] pick up ideas and you have to listen to each other ...

> Adrian: You need to see other people's views
>
> Elisa: ... to be able to get the creative side

Helen, the East of England school partner, said '... the creativity is ... still within me and I've still got it there, it's just a way of drawing it out'. People were working back and forth in conversation between the inside and the outside being stretched into collaborative physical generation. Abi, a South-East England external partner, described 'working from the inside out'. A London student described working in a group with other people and their ideas:

> we were creative with each other because by showing each other our own movements, others were inspired and thought of new and improved ideas. I work in a group and on my own, I think I came out of my comfort zone in the group.

Michael, the East of England external partner, talked about conversing with the artistic idea:

> there is a sense of commitment to the movement which isn't just ... an external thing. I think they were trying to communicate the essence ... they were being ... internally creative there ... I think they'd internalised that ... and I think that that is a creative process because it's about connections between what their body is doing and how's it looking on the outside and awareness of what it feels like.

Students and staff referred to this physical inside-outside conversation and how it stretched them and their ideas. Sarah's group offered and tried out various possibilities to develop the new idea collaboratively, which was ultimately embodied by Sarah and the bridge supporting her.

The inside-outside dialogue

So why is this inside-outside conversation important to the creativity of students like Sarah? Theorising which has stressed the role of dialogue in the artistic and the creative process suggests the answer. Writing about professional dance, Briginshaw discussed the potency of the 'inside/outside interface' (2001:18). She draws on Merleau-Ponty's (1962) idea of the 'double sensation' and Bakhtin's work on dialogue to argue that the interrelation of different views from inside and outside the body has the 'potential for new world views' (Bakhtin, 1984:318). In DPC we are perhaps not seeing new worldviews exactly, but we are seeing new ideas relative to students' peers. These have emerged from physical inside-outside conversations with other people, their ideas and the developing dance idea.

Philosophers have recently begun to consider the inside-out conversation as being pertinent to creativity. Like Briginshaw, and drawing on Merleau-Ponty (1964) and Bakhtin, Wegerif (2010) highlights the importance of dialogue to creativity. He argues that a dialogic relationship is unique because each person is inside the other. It is a sort of 'inside-out' 'outside-in' relationship. The young people in DPC physically crossed each others' boundaries and entered embodied dialogues with their peers and adults in order to generate new collaborative ideas.

Looking further back in philosophy, we find support for embodied dialogue in the work of theoreticians such as John Dewey. He gets to the heart of these physical inter-relations when he says we 'live ... as much in processes across and 'through' skins as in processes 'within' skins' (Dewey in Boydston, Ed, p119).

An embodied process of becoming

The DPC findings reveal that it is not just that the young people were collaboratively developing new ideas but that they themselves were the physical substance of the ideas and so were developing and becoming themselves. They were making and being made. There were numerous visual and verbal references to young people 'becoming' responsible, independent and owning their ideas. One of the best examples comes from the East of England site's Acting Headteacher:

> she's very self conscious ... but I noticed that towards the end of the day she ... was smiling at the visitors, and actually almost trying to catch their eye ... because she wanted, I think, her contribution to be acknowledged ... here was a girl who's really revelling in what she was doing. And I frankly wouldn't have thought that she'd have made that degree of progress.

Just as I had observed the change in Sarah as she crossed the bridge, he saw one of his pupils going through the process of becoming. Abi, a South-East external partner, discussed the importance of 'students becoming artists' and Michael, the East of England external partner, often referred to students 'becoming' more independent, more responsible. The London young people perhaps sum it up best: 'I felt like I have changed', 'I feel creativity is when you expand as an individual'.

Identities developed by doing

Through becoming, young people are 'doing' their identities – what Moje and Luke call developing their 'identity in activity' (p429-431). Sarah became the lynchpin of the group's creative dance idea as she crossed the bridge of hands, and simultaneously became a maker, a performer, the original idea and the answer to the question. Embodied ideas and identities feed each other. Researching professional practice, Moran and John-Steiner (2004) have shown that creativity and identity reciprocally develop each other. The importance of embodiment to this process should not be underestimated. As the body philosopher Shusterman (2008) stated: 'our body constitutes an essential fundamental dimension of our identity ... our dynamic symbiotic selves are constituted by relations with others' (p2).

This underlines the importance of the partnership characteristics of identity shifting and leadership positioning giving young people the freedom to imagine new social positions and identities for themselves. This gives them the power to create new ideas and possibilities. We see the inter-relationship between identity and creativity cyclically completed as they feed each other through the process of becoming.

Humanising creativity – an antidote to sink or swim

Thus humanising creativity engages empathy, shared ownership, risky emotional journeys, negotiating conflict and difference, social responsibility and rigour of artistic intention. And the process involves imagination, exploring multiple possibilities, shared generation and capturing exciting new ideas (Chappell, 2008). The DPC analysis reinforces and builds on all this. What is more, humanising creativity is an embodied process of becoming which is mindful of its consequences. The process is grounded in a reciprocal relationship between the collaborative generation of new ideas and identities development fuelled by ongoing dialogues between inside-out and outside-in.

In Figure 7.4 a mobius strip is used to represent a single continuous surface of connected bodies. If you draw a line with your finger along this strip, you return without interruption to your starting point along the surface. This capacity to keep journeying through bodies and cycling through the inter-action between creativity and identity, between inside and outside, encapsulates the conversation at the heart of humanising creativity and becoming.

The chapter began by asking how humanising creativity and the evidence from DPC challenges the discourse of creativity as marketised and individualised, driven by the performativity agenda and the idea of childhood at risk. As it shows, humanising creativity counters the discourse of marketised, individualised creativity because it does not foreground product and indivi-

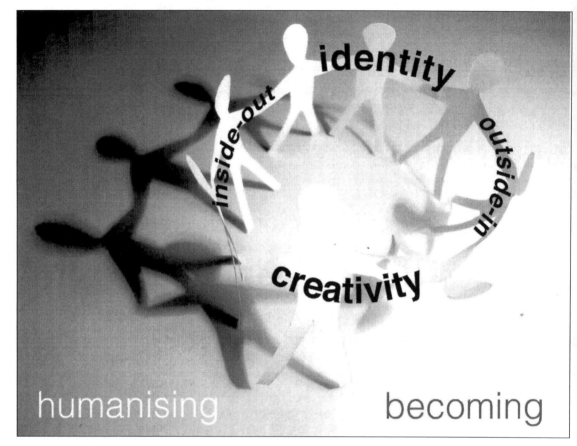

Figure 7.4: Humanising creativity – journeys of becoming

dual generation for their own sake. The DPC evidence shows that partnership is characterised by appropriately flattened hierarchies, by the merger of identity spaces inhabited by adults and students, and it is underpinned by shared social responsibility. It is accompanied by an inside-out/outside-in creative dialogue which is mindful of its communal consequences and which, although working with product, equally values the processes of collaborative creativity and becoming. Creativity is democratic and ethically guided. People creating in this way attend to the development of others and the consequences of their creative actions as much as to their creative ideas.

Humanising creativity values creativity in its own right rather than serving the performativity agenda. The new DPC evidence shows how those involved in creative dance projects become themselves mindfully in partnership, and grow into multiple identities. And process is as vital as product. But this is not anything goes; it is not wishy-washy. Partners in all three sites emphasised the importance of intuitively applied dance knowledge, of professionally-driven artistic intention and rigour that is nonetheless not prescriptive. Where performativity-driven assessment in dance and other subjects might prioritise product characteristics, in DPC sites it is about recognising journeys of becoming, like Sarah's. At times, these were more useful success indicators than the graded quality of dance products fed into school performance data.

Finally, the DPC evidence contradicts the notion of young people at risk and in need of protection. Whilst acting responsibly towards them, it instead reinforces the idea that young people are capable, active and empowered. This is achieved particularly through partnerships which shift power balances, flatten hierarchies and create opportunities to imagine yourself in new identities and leadership roles, within a safe shared group identity. The partnership identity structures support young people as they take responsibility as capable producers, developing and becoming themselves. They are neither passive nor in need of adult protection but can responsibly make judgements about creative direction themselves.

Humanising creativity therefore provides an antidote to the dominant educational discourses which take a sink or swim attitude to young people and which position them as having a survivalist mentality and competing to keep their heads above water. As with other strands of the DPC research, the recent findings and their analysis have implications for practice, theory and policy in terms of the conceptualisation and role of creative partnership in educational futures (considered in Chapter 11). Here, I highlight one emergent finding which seems crucial to both the conception of humanising creativity and to the DPC project's implications for educational futures.

I have made frequent reference to the way that humanising creativity, as illustrated here within dance education, is fundamentally physical and embodied. The dance milieu is one of the best places to see it at work. Partnership relationships were physically and spatially manifested in both the structure and content of the dance sessions. And crucially, the creative process was embodied in young people as the substance of creative ideas; they were making and being made. Shusterman (2008) has argued for a kind of humanism which understands that:

> in our bodily actions we are not self-sufficient agents but stewards and impresarios of larger powers ... the relational self acquires and deploys its powers only through its enabling relations ... and we are ... charged with caring for and harmonising the environmental affordances of our embodied selves. (p214)

Humanising creativity reinforces this argument, making a strong embodied reciprocal connection between our creative ideas, our developing identities and their collaborative, communal and ethical essence. As the capacity for humanising creativity is embodied within us rather than dependent on market forces or targets, it seems to offer far more shared hope for the future than the competitive ethos that pervades our current education system.

8

The development of partnership-based pedagogies

Linda Rolfe

Figure 8.1: Michael and Helen in the East of England site working alongside each other

Introduction

This chapter investigates some of the approaches to teaching used in the partnerships between the Dance Partners for Creativity (DPC) partners and explores how pupils' learning is supported by such pedagogy. Most educators agree that content knowledge, or knowledge of the subject being taught, together with pedagogical knowledge, or techniques for teaching the subject, are essential to support effective learning. In the case of artist-teacher partnerships, as suggested in Chapters 1 and 2, a simplistic approach might create a natural divide, with the artist leading on subject content and the teacher focusing on pedagogy. Speaking from personal experience, this was the most prevalent working method in dance education during the early years of professional dancers and companies working in schools. In the 1970s I participated as a teacher in workshops where my part in the collaboration was at a functional level – that is I 'managed' the pupils and made the organisational arrangements whilst the artist taught a technique workshop based on a piece of repertoire. Probably none of these dancers planned a career in teaching but many, in common with artists today, found themselves teaching at some point in their careers.

Since the early 1980s, an extensive range of education programmes have been developed by dance companies and artists in England, partly because the value of dance in education gained greater recognition. More recently, research by Castle *et al* (2002) found that dance companies with education programmes viewed 'working with teachers as problematic' (p96). One reason these authors gave is that when working within the limitations of dance placed in the physical education (PE) curriculum there was over-reliance on formulae. They also identified a need to improve their understanding of education initiatives and how best to work with teachers. The long-standing debate surrounding dance as part of PE in the English school curriculum continues (eg Jobbins, 1999).

My training as a dance teacher in London had prepared me to be an educator and this influenced my artistic work in dance. My opportunities to engage in choreography and performance outside my teaching context diminished, as it was governed by the school curriculum. This was true for a present-day teacher located in London, who asked: 'Can I be both a teacher and artist?' (Jeffery, 2005:8). DPC asks similar questions and in this chapter I investigate how partnership pedagogies have developed over time and what theoretical frameworks might inform them.

Areas of research

Two research areas have informed my exploration of partnership pedagogies. The one relating to understanding partnership includes Jeffery (2005), who maps out four complementary dimensions of artist-teacher partnership (see Chapter 9). Much of the literature places an emphasis on the artist's role and views their work as an intervention from the outside (Pringle, 2008). Such partnerships are identified as shifting 'learning into the border zone between the worlds of education, culture and communities' (Jeffery and Ledgard, 2009:6).

The second area is conceptualisations about communities of practice. For Wenger, 'the difference between a community of practice and any social network is that social relations are formed, negotiated and sustained around the activity that has brought people together' (Fuller, 2007:21). Wenger (1998:72) identifies three dimensions which form the basis 'by which practice is the source of coherence of a community':

- the mutual engagement of participants which involves doing things together so that being included in what matters is a requirement for being engaged in a community's practice
- a joint enterprise which is defined as a process, not a static agreement which produces relations of mutual accountability, which pushes practice forwards and invites new ideas
- a shared repertoire whereby shared histories of engagement can become resources for negotiating meaning without the need to constantly 'compare notes'

The influence and energy that can be generated through a community of practice can challenge and transform, for example, the demands of an institution or models of working (Wenger, 1998). Recognising their existence therefore has the potential to inform pedagogical practice within the education system and more specifically in dance education. One way to analyse and transform such behaviours is through investigating the community of practice to which teachers belong. Griffiths and Woolf (2004) make the point in relation to artists and teachers entering the community of practice of the other practitioner, where there are permeable boundaries. So applying the notion of community of practice to partnerships may help us to explore how divisions, conflicts and struggles affect the possibilities of crossing boundaries for artists/teachers, and act as a catalyst for creativity (Jeffery, 2005).

The partnership literature reports that the territories occupied by teachers and artists are shaped by complex power relationships and include misunderstandings and myths which need to be interrogated (Jeffery and Ledgard, 2009). My DPC focus is on how pedagogy can be informed by questioning the perceived boundaries and understanding the nuances we possibly take for granted. The teaching approaches used across the three DPC sites is my first focus, and draws on dance teaching literature. This is followed by suggestions about how partnerships opened up new possibilities for teaching and the contribution made to participants' professional development. The chapter concludes with a discussion of how partnership pedagogy can be informed by the dimensions of communities of practice (Wenger, 1998).

Teaching approaches
A journey of discovery

Evidence showed that partners were all mutually engaged in their projects and viewed it as a joint enterprise. It was clear, however, that they started from different interpretations of the impetus for the work. This is probably no surprise given the school context. The driving force for the external partners tended to be an artistic vision, as Bim from the London site explained: '... I don't think about their learning ... My starting point is an artistic vision' (London site, beginning of project).

Caroline, the school partner, was very aware of the need to prepare the pupils for dance examinations and the whole school agenda. The external partner had less responsibility for the students' learning so could focus on what was required to create imaginative and new choreography, as reflected in the following conversation:

> Caroline: ... but I would still be honed into can these children talk about it? Can they express it? Have they developed it? To what level have they developed it? ... what about their performance, what about ... all the skills that they're meant to have.
>
> Linda: Can I ask Bim then, are you thinking about those things?
>
> Bim: No, I'm thinking about are they fully engaged with the task in the class, really important. Are they being careful of people around them? And are they making work that's interesting? And if they're not what tools do I need to give them to make their work interesting? (London site, beginning of project)

The external partners in the three sites focused on the artistic process with an emphasis on venturing into new and challenging areas of dance experience, as described by Michael, in the East of England, part way through the project:

> that sense of mystery ... where's this going to go ... and that sense of surprise and mystery and the cliff-hanger of next week we'll carry on. I think all that's really important to this sort of work to keep them engaged and interested and not tell them what's going to happen ... you haven't said by the end of the lesson you will all be able to do X, Y and Z.

In these comments there is a sense of the choreography voyaging into the unknown and a recognition of how the teaching approaches engage pupils and capture their interest in learning. This is corroborated by one of the pupils in the South-East England site, at the end of project:

> It's good because she [external partner] pushes us, and you never know like obviously where you're going to finish ... I want to do it for myself and everybody else, but you ... also want to push yourself for Abi and Carrie [external partners] as well.

Creating new possibilities

The sense of a voyage of discovery allowed the partners to make the most of opportunities as they arose. They talked in two sites about not planning tightly how they would teach but of interacting with each other and the pupils. The teaching approaches were not clearly delineated between the two partners as they reflected in action and responded to situations which arose. This reflects earlier research (Craft, 2008b) and aligns closely with Wenger's views,

> Teaching must be opportunistic because it cannot control its own effects. Opportunism does not mean laissez-faire ... what matters is ... the ability for teaching and learning to interact so as to become structuring resources for each other. (Wenger, 1998:267)

This implies that there is a map for the journey but that different routes are possible. In dance education, routes include a combination of problem-solving teaching approaches and direct teaching methods (eg Gough, 1999). The external partners in the three DPC initiatives had knowledge of different kinds about the learners. They were collaborating and sharing their expertise with the school partners in order to plan an open-ended structure for the project.

The mutual engagement of partners allowed for complementary approaches to emerge drawing on what partners do and know, as well as connecting with what they don't do or know. This giving and sharing of knowledge became a resource for teaching which was further strengthened by the overlapping competences that existed between the partners. There are different ways to approach partnership planning but openness and a willingness to allow teaching approaches to emerge during the process ensured a dynamic learning environment. The new ideas that emerged through the joint enterprise of teaching in partnership reflect what Jeffery (2005) refers to as the artistry of teaching.

Co-construction of choreography

The dance-making involved the partners in establishing teaching methods which valued collaborative choreography with pupils actively engaged in, for example, exploring ideas, using their imagination to solve problems, and structuring movement material. There was very little teaching of movement created by the external partner. The following quote is from a school partner in the South-East of England site, mid-project, where the teaching involved the external partner working alongside the pupils:

> The bravery to work in absolute partnership, you absolutely trust them [the pupils] to create movement material, even when it doesn't look quite right.

Part of the external partners' teaching approach was to share skills and expertise as they worked alongside the pupils to co-construct the choreography. The sessions were characterised by setting open tasks which encouraged pupils to explore movement responses and generate their own vocabulary. In Figure 8.2 pupils from the South-East of England site are working in pairs to create a phrase based on imagery.

In all the DPC sites both the partners demonstrated a shared understanding of the practice of making dances, involving collaborative learning through discussion and dialogue. The worlds of professional dance and dance education adopt similar practices when creating choreography. Many professional choreographers involve dancers in actively making work, using processes that dance teachers would understand and be able to incorporate into their repertoire of teaching (eg Bannerman *et al*, 2006). These processes involve for example: improvisation around tasks, teaching movement vocabulary, using specified dance techniques and styles, and making reference to the current professional dance repertoire. These artistic processes are well documented in published interviews with choreographers, documentaries about making dance and dance education resource packages. An external partner in the South-East of England site, mid-project, explains their choreographic processes:

Figure 8.2: Pupils working in pairs to create an imagery-based phrase

> The making process is ... through the students composing their own movement material, or at the very least developing material that Lîla Dance teach to them ... much of their material is created in response to tasks, feedback, images ... the process becomes entirely applicable to their own practises at school.

The transfer of learning

The connection between choreographic practice in the project and the school strengthens the common territory that exists between the partners and makes the transfer of learning easier. It recognises the need to increase pupil's ability to reflect on their learning and develop critical-thinking skills (eg Lavender, 1996). A strength of the partnerships was a shared approach to teaching choreography as they worked together using a common spoken and physical language of dance. There were, however, some subtle differences between how the partners expressed the movement tasks. In the London site, for example, Bim, the external partner, described her mid-project approach:

> I think the way I encourage students to learn is through asking them open ended questions like how could you do that differently or what could make that more exciting.

This differed from the approach of her school partner, Caroline, as described by the university researcher when she reflected on a lesson:

> Caroline explains why they are doing the task, use of space and body parts, asks questions of pupils, breaks task down and layers how they might answer the task.

Her reflection on another lesson in London notes that:

> Bim insists that they try using different body parts, calls out 'carve a road through your kinesphere' asks for ideas for pathways through space, a pupil calls out 'a square' and they all try that idea. Caroline suggests how to connect the movements, only time that she takes a lead role.

These examples highlight a teaching approach which was seen across the three sites, where the external partners tended to leave the pupils more space, physically and mentally, when solving movement problems. They used language to encourage pupils to strive for original outcomes; they used imagery and prompted them to give ideas. School partners were more inclined to suggest possible ways to answer the task by the use of, for example, action, space or dynamics. They also used imagery and involved pupils in answering questions but their focus appeared to be more on the learning process than on artistic outcomes. As the projects developed over time the partners began to reflect together and share approaches, for example when setting tasks as in this conversation:

> Bim: ... instead of saying to your students use a different level, say to them distort your body posture to get out of the way.
>
> Caroline: Yes, and I would say that.
>
> Bim: That's much more open.
>
> (London site, end of project)

Not all the ideas worked, as sometimes the tasks were not close enough to the pupils' prior experience and took them outside their comfort zone. For example tasks that were very abstract involving the exploration of movement concepts with few prompts could produce poor results and possibly lead to behaviour problems. This might then lead the partners to take a different teaching approach and set another task, or just persevere to see what happened.

The repertoire of choreographic practice

The curriculum model for dance in schools refers to professional dance works which are at the cutting edge of choreography. This lack of a divide between contemporary dance and choreography in schools, together with an overlapping understanding of choreographic approaches, allowed the partners to use this shared history as a resource for developing new ways of teaching.

Whilst the partners shared points of reference, such as terminology, concepts and dance works, they also experienced some differences in meaning, for example setting open tasks in choreography. This provided the opportunity to share their interpretation of well-established ideas and in dialogue to reaffirm them or take them in unexpected directions. Wenger (1998) recognises the potential of this feature of a shared repertoire of practice to develop new meanings and views it as a resource rather than a constraint on practice. Sharing routines, words or ways of doing things was not a strong feature when I was working as a dance teacher with dance artists, which may reflect the emerging state of contemporary dance in the professional world of the 1970s in England. The art of choreography was still rooted in a traditional didactic approach to teaching ballet repertoire with the choreographer creating work on the dancers rather than with them. The artistry of teaching as outlined by Jeffery (2005) was in my experience also sadly lacking, with little dialogue between myself and the dance artist.

Ways of working: new possibilities for teaching
Demonstration

The partnerships opened up possibilities to teach in different ways. They were able to physically demonstrate choreographic ideas, for example using lifts and contact, which pupils could observe, discuss and try for themselves. When partners were dancing with each other, pupils could see ideas being explored and the physical risks involved. Physical demonstration seems to generate great interest and enthusiasm in pupils for learning, as the activities connect personally with them. Providing models of the completed task, such as a movement motif or a concept such as suspension, gave pupils an oppor-tunity to observe and develop a conceptual model of the task or process before attempting to perform it. The learning power of live demonstration in dance provided a model of what might be possible and how to work colla-boratively with another person. The demonstrations provided a compelling example of working relationships in dance which are a key element in certain choreography.

Part way through the project pupils in the London site supported this saying:

> Bim and Miss Watkins worked together very well and when they were demonstrating they improvised very well.

> I thought that they were best friends.

> They help us feel more comfortable and confident.

> They work together well. They discuss and make it happen. They are equal.

Collaborative learning

Dance requires personal exploration and collaboration as integral parts of the artistic process (see Chapter 7) and the DPC sites contain abundant evidence of pupils working collaboratively as choreographers. This is not a feature in all art forms; for example the visual arts may be quite solitary (Jeffery and Ledgard, 2009). The partners became role models as both the external and school partners moved away from teacher-centred instruction towards a shared understanding of working as dancers alongside the pupils. In the London site it was Bim, the external partner, who continually pushed Caroline, the school partner, to work as a choreographer with an artistic vision for the project. Letting go of familiar ways of working meant that Caroline allowed the artistic process to be in the foreground. It also required Bim to let go of some artistic responsibility, which she found a challenge but rewarding. They shared a collaborative approach to choreography with the pupils which required re-thinking and refining their pedagogy.

The London site partners were learning from each other and this was a very strong element in this site. Bim felt that previously she had not entered a partnership expecting to use the teacher's expertise or consider what she might learn. In this project it was different and she learnt from Caroline as shown in their discussion at the end of the project:

> Bim: I don't think artists use the teacher's expertise. I mean obviously I'm working with somebody like top-end ... what can I learn from you, and actually I've got heaps I can learn from you. But because of how artists are defined and how teachers are defined, particularly in this relationship, that is just not in the equation usually.

> ... is it not also about sharing and developing one's expertise between two professionals?

> Caroline: Your creativity and the way that maybe ... I work with the kids might be different in the way that you do, and you might learn new skills.

> Bim: Right.

They are open to creating new understandings by going outside the boundaries of their normal teaching approach and lesson content. Being exposed to new ideas encouraged all the school partners to take a fresh look at their teaching. What Helen, school partner in the East of England site said at the beginning of project is typical:

> I'm exposed to new ideas, and it's sparking off my creativity and making me want to go away and think about things that I am doing in lessons and perhaps revisiting them in a new light.

Evolving communities of practice through partnership

The term community of practice has been applied to the worlds of both teaching and partnership (Griffiths and Woolf, 2004; Jeffery and Ledgard, 2009; Jeffery, 2005) and its influence and the implications of its ideas have relevance for DPC. The characteristics which follow seem to align closely with Wenger's indicators which revolve around the nature and quality of social relations and interaction, and their links to practice. The three dimensions of a community of practice – a community of mutual engagement, a joint enterprise and a shared repertoire (Wenger, 1998) – were significantly present in the project. Partnerships provided enormous potential for involvement in a joint enterprise between the worlds of dance and education. Ways of working together crossed perceived boundaries between communities to challenge preconceived models and embrace new ideas. This suggests that we can better understand the pedagogy if we recognise the elements that can strengthen it through consciously creating communities of practice.

It emerged as important for both kinds of partners that they embody the art form of dance in the teaching approaches they shared. This entailed teachers using their artistic understanding of dance to inform their pedagogy so they felt connected to the subject. They provided students with access to greater understanding of dance by becoming or embodying a role as choreographer, performer and critic (see Chapter 7). This view of active participation in the subject is emphasised by Wenger (1998) as essential for teaching.

Partnerships can be perceived as both an intervention and collaboration. There exist different kinds of cultural practice which need to be better understood. As one DPC partner put it: 'it opened doors through our collaboration'. We need to recognise that although there are cultural differences between the two worlds, if partnership is seen as collaboration (Jeffery and Ledgard, 2009), partners can take pupils on a learning journey, not by doing the same as each other but through embracing diversity.

The artist, teacher and pupils all bring their experience and knowledge from outside the project but these overlap as they interact. Wenger (1998) stresses that adults need to 'invite' pupils into their ways of working. Adults are able to model ways of working in dance for pupils which allows them to be a part of the activity and invites them into a community of practice. The co-construction of choreography involves a pedagogy carrying challenges and responsibilities that gives pupils greater ownership and calls on the knowledge of students by encouraging them to explore new territories.

A commitment by partners and pupils to the project was evident in all three sites, but this was constantly worked at in order to engage everyone. The partners had to work at their relationships and those they created with the pupils. Even though the partners had common dance backgrounds they had to negotiate a range of practicable teaching approaches suitable for the context, subject content and learners. Recognising the complexity involved in order to realise the potential of all participants takes time and the willingness to collaborate. DPC has certainly opened up new possibilities for pedagogy which extend far beyond my experience of partnerships in the 1970s. In this project the partnerships benefited from enough continuity for participants to develop shared practices and a long term commitment to the enterprise and each other.

9

Becoming meddlers in the middle:
stretch, challenge and leap?

Anna Craft

... it is time for 'unlearning' old teaching habits – the habits of the Sage and the Guide, and engaging in a new learning habit – the habit of being a Meddler.' (McWilliam, 2008:268)

I learned from Bim, that you can be silly in dancing and have fun but you have to be serious when it comes to improving. (Comment by pupil at London site, end of project)

Dance Partners for Creativity (DPC) nurtured teachers and dance practitioners in combining enjoyment with improvement, creativity with high standards – as signalled by the student above. At its heart was research-focused creative partnership to develop pedagogy and learning (see Chapter 8) using the lens of community of practice. In this chapter, I consider how the enquiry strand amplified what McWilliam (2008) calls 'meddling in the middle', and so opened up 'possibility spaces'.

In our initiatives in schools with 11-14 year olds, we aimed to nurture student creativity through partnership (see Chapters 1 and 2). We were acknowledging two competing cultures: the creative culture of nurturing possibility, and the performative culture of students' achievements being used as measures not only of students' worth but also of schools' success. Performativity, a term coined by Ball (2003), is in tension with creativity (see eg Bragg *et al*, 2009; Galton, 2008; Thomson *et al*, 2009). Through co-participative research design we hoped to soften boundaries and open dynamic space for exploration of both aspects of practice. This nurtured lively dialogue in which perspectives were inhabited and shared; 'living dialogic space' (Chappell and Craft, in press) in which partners engaged in creative learning conversations, enabling differences to be heard and recognised.

As previous chapters show, our partners co-researched through extensively artistic and reflective approaches to creative partnership. Jeffery (2005) discusses four complementary artist-teacher partnership approaches:

- Teacher as artist: creative teacher practices (personal and institutional)
- Artist as educator: artist working at boundary of formal/less formal learning
- Artistry of teaching: pedagogy fuelled, developed by reflection on practice
- Artistic work as model and educator: making works of art as tools, models

In the three DPC sites with school and external partner relationships, the partners co-developed classroom pedagogy, privileging different dimensions of Jeffery's partnership practices at different times. The development of pedagogy was therefore bound up in research collaboration. And we came to understand this research-pedagogy mesh as 'meddling in the middle' (McWilliam, 2008).

Meddling in the middle

McWilliam (2008) first used this term to describe the changing role of the teacher. She argued that in past times teachers were seen as sage-on-the-stage (as experts, filling up novice students with knowledge and skills) then, in the late 20th century, as guide-on-the-side (coaching students, recognising their existing knowledge and experience). But, in a world in which digital technologies enable de-routinisation, co-construction and co-authoring in the workplace and in social interaction, pedagogy needs to be much more creative. McWilliam's concept of teacher as meddler (2008:265) challenges teachers to:

- Recognise it is not possible to 'know' it all and to therefore spend more time 'being a usefully ignorant co-worker in the thick of the action'
- Recognise the vital role of risk in today's world, prioritising this over being a 'custodial risk minimiser'

–   Enter into designing, assembling and editing alongside students rather than being a 'forensic classroom auditor'

–   Move beyond counselling into being 'a collaborative critic and authentic evaluator'

We found strong resonances in DPC. Our partners engaged readily with one another, perhaps reflecting their experience of the long tradition within the arts of valuing interaction. We documented partner researchers in DPC:

■   recognising the role of uncertainty and not-knowing

■   acknowledging the vital role of risk-taking

■   designing, assembling, editing together with university researchers

■   actively co-engaging with university researchers as evaluators and critics

These characteristics can be seen in two examples. One is a midway reflection by the external partner in the London site, where research focused on how the school and external partners developed their practice: '... normally when I go in as an artist I have a goal, it is the performance ... the skills that you need for a performance are quite different to the skills you need to be creative ... what was exciting about [this project] was the creative process ...' She went on to discuss their collaboration – characterised as risky, collaborative and dynamic: '... we were quite risky, weren't we, with our physicality which also had an impact on the way [the students] approached the creative work ... I think it opened doors ... it was actually a very creative process between us two ...'

She saw this aspect of their collaboration as vital to how they nurtured creativity in students by acting as role models co-constructing, co-designing and co-critiquing:

> ... part of the reason this project was so successful was not me, it was the collaboration, because the students saw their teacher who was their role model working incredibly closely with somebody on the outside ... because of that they were really, really brave ... Which I think is fundamental to creativity because you have to not be scared to go into the unknown ...

This was corroborated by her school partner: '... we'd empowered the students to such an extent that they were actually commanding their own creativity and structuring their own work ...'. Students too recognised the difference, which left them feeling as one student put it: 'Flow to be more creative and confident with myself'. Earlier in the term, another student had said, '... it's a little bit different because here we get to do what we want and we just don't sit and listen. She ... talks for like one minute then she's like – okay that's what we're going to do ...'

Adopting this meddling in the middle practice, partners co-engaged in numerous ways, as shown in the images in Figure 9.1a and b. And as the quotations suggest, their meddling permeated their classroom practice and, it seemed, the students' creativity.

Above: Figure 9.1a and right: 9.1b: Bim and Caroline in conversation in contrasting ways

The second example comes from the South-East England site, where dynamism and critique inherent in researchful partnership was highlighted by one external partner: '... joining, contrasting or meeting of minds ... the contrasting bit is important ... you have to argue sometimes to get to the next point. So we often have ... mini little arguments ... and then we both go away and think about it and then come to an answer'. This is reflected by a representation drawn out in a mapping task by her school partner highlighting the theme of 'Trusting in each other ... Openness to difference, that's all about trust isn't it?' She emphasises dialogue and difference moving to agreed action: 'Joining ... contrasting ... meeting of minds ... Compromise'. She highlights the openness in the research: '... I've done projects before where I feel very much like this is our question, we want this answer please ... [in DPC] ... you don't want a strict answer ... just ... more questions ...'

In DPC, working with uncertainty, taking risks, co-creating and co-engaging in critique were vital features of creative learning conversations (see Chapter 2). Theorisation of dialogue involved in creative learning conversations is undertaken elsewhere (Chappell and Craft, in press). What this chapter does is to frame the action-oriented co-research in terms of the powerful learning dynamic in the relationship, as meddling with possibility.

Meddling in the middle of possibility space

The researchful partnerships of DPC opened up 'possibility spaces' (Craft, 2010). They made opportunities to act or behave 'as if', so as to nurture creativity among 11-14 year olds. School and external partners developed dimensions of their practice as both artists and teachers, working alongside one another and the students to make authentic dance works of art. Teachers inhabited the artist in themselves, artists inhabited their educator persona. Each partner co-explored their extended identities:

> School partner: ... [at the beginning] I was a bit more ... teacher-like ... I was thinking about the practical side of things ...

> External partner: as the process went on ... definitely myself as an artist, my voice, became less and less important ... it was more about the collective ...

> School partner: Yes, definitely ... (London site, end of project)

Partners thus explored the artistry of teaching, developing and theorising pedagogy through their research. As co-investigators, they actively constructed meanings in developing learning and pedagogy in the classroom. They acted 'as if' they were researchers in what for some became a profound learning experience.

All the usual expectations of creative partnership were thrown in the air, and a space opened. In the East of England site the school partner concentrated on observing and supporting the external partner in the dance sessions. She was able to concentrate on students' experiences:

> stepping out of it [i.e. teaching] ... I could see one [student] ... was really quite nervous about working on her own. But ... having taught her ... it strikes me that she needs to be pushed, and the more things that she's being pushed in, the more things that she has excelled in and begun to enjoy ...

This was challenging, but it yielded insights. Partners began questioning, justifying and judging their personal views and practices, in dialogue with themselves and their partners, sometimes feeling exposed and vulnerable. This opened a Pandora's box for some school partners in particular for whom fitting in to the school system had meant shedding or silencing some of their artistic beliefs, values and behaviour. As the school partner in the London site said part-way through their collaboration,

> I have to know that they've understood the task, the process they've gone through and that they can talk about it and that they can demonstrate what they've learned at a more complex level ... because that's what Ofsted want me to do ... I have to be very ... methodical about how I go about it, but the way that we're going about it I'm trying to be more the artist.

Reflecting with her external partner later, reveals frustration:

> School partner: I have to tie in all manner of different things from ... being able ... to speak about their experiences and evaluate and target set and then actually write about it ... I've got so many different things that I have to build into it ... I have to work like that.
>
> External partner: Yeah.
>
> School partner: I find that sometimes quite rigid ... sometimes I just want to be a bit more abstract and a bit more ...
>
> External partner: Free, yeah.
>
> School partner: I want to see what comes out of it [the project].
>
> External partner: Yeah, yeah.

Engaging in research oriented partnership demanded courage, uncovering buried values. Together, partners in each site opened possibility space for developing and interrogating classroom practice.

Stretching

Meddling in the middle opened new ways of engaging with dance teaching. Our analysis revealed tensions between the perspectives and experience of various partners. Some felt intensely stretched. As the external partner in the London site said, it 'feels risky – on the edge'. There were four main dimensions in which partners were stretched.

Research

DPC stretched people beyond customary creative partnership, to research-focused endeavour. Being co-researching partners, felt unfamiliar to most. It brought to the fore a powerful reflective process, interpreted by some as the opportunity to break rules. As the external partner in the London site said as the project finished: '... right from the beginning we established ... We're going to break the rules ...'. In their site, where their focus was their own practice, this meant they had to investigate the process of their partnership through creativity.

Collective endeavour

Whatever the site-specific research question, data collection and analysis required the participants to be part of a larger organism. As the external partner in the East of England site said at the close of the project, the '... sum of the parts is greater ... complimentarity ... a support network moving towards a common goal'. The research focus meant developing trust in co-reflecting. Earlier on, this external partner had observed: '... it's not necessarily that it's all planned and in detail and everything's up front, but more about ... trust what the other can bring, or take a risk with that ... go with it ...'

Fluidity

Trust and reflection demanded fluidity. In the East of England site, the partners had worked together before. This time, the research angle allowed the school partner to step back and observe. Reflecting toward the end of the project, she said,

> ... the impact that it has on me is as great [as it is on the students] ... observing has been as interesting as being part of [it] and actually thinking about what the students are getting out of it. In previous years with a project, I've been able to work to enjoy it but ... considering the purpose of the project in a more detailed way is making me appreciate its full worth.

She highlighted the open-endedness of the research, experiencing this as creative: 'Part of what I enjoy ... is stepping into the unknown. It's allowing me to express a sense of creativity ...' In the same site, the external partner had worked with the university researcher as part of her doctoral study but not as co-researcher. The transition into collaboration led the three of them to work together in new ways.

Framing dance teaching

The partners' involvement in co-researching pedagogy stretched most school partners to experiment with looser framing of dance teaching. This final stretch appeared to offer students a more creative experience. As one pupil half way through the London project, put it:

> ... it's different because in this half term we had fun. It was actually fun doing the dance. But for the other half term, yeah, ... Miss ... would give us a dance to do. We can do our own crazy stuff ... We actually just stand up and work together ...

Yet school partners were acutely aware of encountering constraints. In the London site, the school partner described usual lessons as

> ... bite-sized, not a journey ... [it] comes back to this, having to break everything down and be so careful to include all those things ... because ultimately you want the kids ... progressing through from Y10 right through to the end of Y13, having opted for your subject ... I do sometimes feel ... very bogged down with that ...

This led on to a conversation:

> External partner: yeah, whereas ... .I guess I don't have that?
>
> School partner 'You don't have that? You don't have that'.
>
> External partner 'I guess that's what artists bring as well is that I don't feel bogged down by anything'.

On the whole, school partners felt they should know their journey and destination. External partners were generally more willing to be spontaneous, adaptable, responsive. In the South-East England site, one external partner suggested early on that: 'being a true artist ... is ... first of all to allow yourself to go into chaos, but always be able to draw yourself back ... .', but this perspective was countered by one of her school partners, who argued that as a teacher, she felt constraint had an important role, and that the rigour of the art form should be visibly demonstrated:

> ... [students] ... need quite a close task and lots of rules to help them create ... I know in terms of teaching and ... we have to convince people that it is about rigour, focus, repetition, reflection, thought ...

The four different aspects which stretched roles and perspectives reflect differentiated characteristics of artists and teachers, as documented elsewhere (eg Burnard and Swann, 2010; Galton, 2008; Griffiths and Woolf, 2004; Pringle, 2008). Studies have highlighted artists' and teachers' approaches and motivations nested in everyday working environments and requirements from wider school and national priorities.

Our partners' priorities, roles and ways of working in this research-focused work suggested a different model. Rather than being characterised in terms of polarised difference (eg Galton, 2008; Pringle, 2008), a multi-dimensional metaphor seems appropriate: different parties play distinctive, dynamically shifting and rotating roles in the whole.

One partnership raised the metaphor of family. They referred, for example, to the university researcher as mother figure, viewing themselves as children who were nearly ready to leave home and lead independent lives yet wanting to keep in touch.

At the end of the project in the East of England, the school partner represented it as a journey of many travellers. This extract illustrates the sensitivity to experiences within and beyond DPC:

> School partner: I've got a big red thing going off my line going up high towards the top ... which is very late nights with [project documentation] ... another red blob straight after which is stress and work goes up very high. And yours [addressed to university researcher] is escalating and getting higher and higher and leans over the top of mine. It kind of evens off but stays up very high.

> University researcher: That's probably about right, yeah.

> School partner: That's pregnancy as well in there ... then Michael and Linda have got overlapping peaks that move towards CORD [external presentation]. Then Michael and my lines go off straight ... I've just drawn a massive red peaking because I know ... it will be a really stressful time ... Veronica's got a little peak in here because she's obviously involved in CORD ... it says stress, work, conversations, meeting by phone ...

Partners developed complementary roles. The school partner quoted above said, mid-project, that she saw her role as 'getting [students] to consider how they can be creative independently [of adult-determined direction]'. The opportunity to work and research together allowed her to focus on that process dimension. Consequently 'he [external partner] might be thinking about the final outcome whereas I'd be thinking about the process of getting to it'. Relationships were intense; the research teams becoming close during colla-

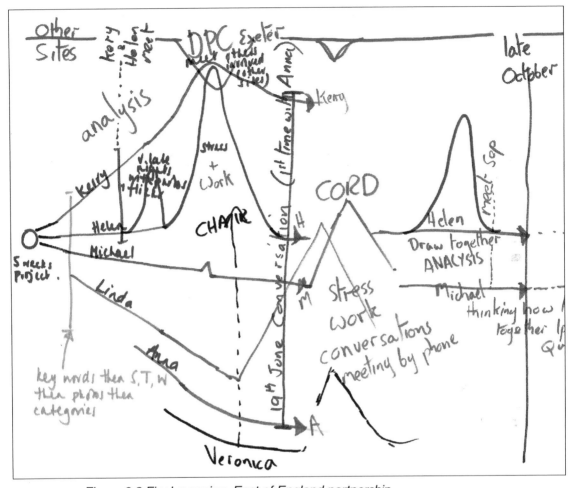

Figure 9.2 Final mapping, East of England partnership

boration, illustrated in this conversation between external partner and university researcher when the project ended:

> School partner: Are we still allowed to send you the occasional little hello.
>
> University researcher: Absolutely, of course, yes.
>
> School partner: It seems a shame to lose contact ... we've worked so closely ... I'd love to know how you get on.

Thus as partners strove to foster both excellence and creativity, these intense, stretching, shifting and complementary roles in each site contributed to collaborative yet differentiated engagement.

Challenging practice and research

There were also challenges. Among them was determining which persona guides practice. School partners talked about classroom discipline. So did external partners, whilst recognising that as dance artists they needed teaching skills to relate to non-dance specialist students ... Yet there were differences: at the project end, the external partner in the London site reflected, '... I don't feel like I *have* to do anything, and I think that's a huge difference about the way we approach something ...' whilst her partner said of her own approach as determined by her responsibilities as a teacher, '... I've got so many different things that I have to build into it ... I find that sometimes quite rigid ...'. Yet she felt the openness that they themselves modelled, led the students to excel: '... they all had something which was amazing that they brought about for themselves that I've never seen before as a result of this project ...'. Comparing this to what students normally produced, both partners regretted that collaboration had revealed future ground to cover:

> School partner: ... I'm only disappointed with what I see there, I'm not at all disappointed with what they've experienced or what they've learned from the whole situation because it's just, it's phenomenal what they've gained from it and empowered them to be able to do.

> External partner: ... I think all of us have that experience including us as practitioners ... everybody went through a similar process ...

In this case, each partner worked differently from their usual way. The project gave them permission to break rules and at the same time, examine how they did it. The external partner reflected on the way encouraging spontaneity rather than adhering to pre-agreed fixed outcomes, enabled creativity rather than fixed outcomes, describing this challenging of their usual practices as initially confusing and even dispiriting, but later as 'exciting'.

How researching and reflecting affected partners' perceptions of partnership was a related challenge. This could produce new understandings. In the South-East England site, partners reflected on their preparations for a presentation toward the end of the project.

> External partner 1: Making a presentation actually articulates your thoughts ...
> External partner 2: It's a step
> External partner 1: It's a revelation ...
> University researcher: A critical moment
> School researcher: It was though, it was a critical moment, ... a high point ...
> University researcher 2: Put a light bulb ...

> School partner: Eureka. I've got to draw a light bulb

Researching could sometimes intensify and magnify the participants' discomfort. In the London site, the external partner reported feeling 'freaked out completely' at the start. At the end, she reflected uncomfortably on having disciplined a student for leaning against the wall:

> External partner: Yeah but … That's a teacher role
>
> School partner: Yes, it IS a teacher role
>
> External partner: … and that's what's interesting
>
> School partner: It is a teacher role
>
> External partner: … that's what's interesting … because me today disciplining, that is definitely being a teacher … not being the artist …

Her school partner found herself, mid-project, envying her partner's greater freedom:

> … it's made me question a little bit about what I do compared to what you do … it's made me feel quite jealous in some ways that I haven't got the luxury to have the opportunity to explore, like you have … My role as a teacher is far more rigid … I'm governed by … restraints of … curriculum and … assessments …

Daring to leap?

In each site, DPC opened spaces of possibility with stretches and challenges. Practice was transformed, partners and students were developed when they achieved previously unattainable goals by working together in practical and reflective exploration of diverse perspectives. The projects prompted positive reactions from other staff:

> … word has got round that this is credible … frankly, we wouldn't hesitate to repeat what was done via the dance project … the skill level, the enthusiasm, the confidence, the commitment are rising … we've gone from … where we almost had to persuade, plead, cajole individuals to go into productions … there is a natural expectation now that there will be productions, and … a thirst for that experience. (Head, East of England, at project's end)

Partners were intensely aware of dynamics of power, authority and engagement in dance teaching, and in creative partnership practice. Meddling in the middle was unique in each site, enabling a variety of ways of actively engaging in making change, or transforming *what is* to *what might be*.

Interestingly, this meddling approach may now sit at a fulcrum of change. Strongly co-creative, it contrasts with educational policy change in England where this study was undertaken. The Coalition government is pulling back from creativity toward performativity. It is withdrawing from co-creation and re-connecting with adult expertise and, perhaps most worryingly, identifying what core knowledge they see as necessary to a rounded secondary school education. This appears to exclude the arts (DfE, 2010; Institute of Education, 2011).

The White Paper on Education, *The Importance of Teaching* (DfE, 2010) signals a new era in pedagogy, with the possibility of re-introducing policy support for McWilliam's caricatured sage-on-the-stage who fills empty vessels with knowledge, at the expense of the guide-on-the-side who helps learners to discover. In this new framing of school learning, it is not yet clear whether there is any role for pedagogy characterised by meddling in the middle.

DPC illustrated how research-focused creative partnership can enable daring creativity in not only students but in everyone involved in teaching and learning, and how it can maximise the authenticity and dynamism offered by professional dance practitioners working with students. As the London site external partner observed at the project's conclusion: '... what the difference was, and what was exciting ... was watching [students] go from comfort to something quite beyond anything they had ever dared explore ...' A student confirmed this, saying: '... I've learned how to dance openly and freely and how to explore new ideas without feeling embarrassed ...'

The world beyond education is entering a global phase of open collective innovation. It is possible (through web-based social networking and content generating) for large numbers of people to produce and refine innovative ideas in response to rapid change by using flexibility, ingenuity and creativity. Yet education, at least in England, is in danger of trudging backward into hierarchically-controlled stasis.

It is time for leaping. DPC offers a magnifying lens on how creativity and excellence can be co-developed. In the words of a primary Head whose final year pupils participated in the East of England partnership:

> I really was overwhelmed ... I still feel close to tears now ... because of the professionalism of the children ... not a giggle ... not a smirk. They ... undertook it as a completely professional exercise ... the way they've all worked together, and remembered all their moves and the lines they created ... everything was perfect ... it was all just spot on ... it was that professional, you would not have minded going to see that and paying money for it ... it was that good.

The site's external partner summed up the aspirations for her students: '... to connect the physical and the imaginative ... that extra leap of engagement ... that's a very creative act, not the creative building of the work but the performance with the intention'.

Working together to be 'spot on', to be 'completely professional', and to produce something novel and inspirational, means being brave enough to leap beyond what we already know how to do as educators and learners. It does not mean trudging backward to a known territory of reproducing the past.

Leaping demands familiarity with known boundaries, sensitivity to what might be appropriate next, and confidence and capability in journeying into new territories with others. Part 4 considers what DPC's methodology and findings could mean for co-creating educational futures.

PART FOUR
FROM WHAT IS TO WHAT MIGHT BE...

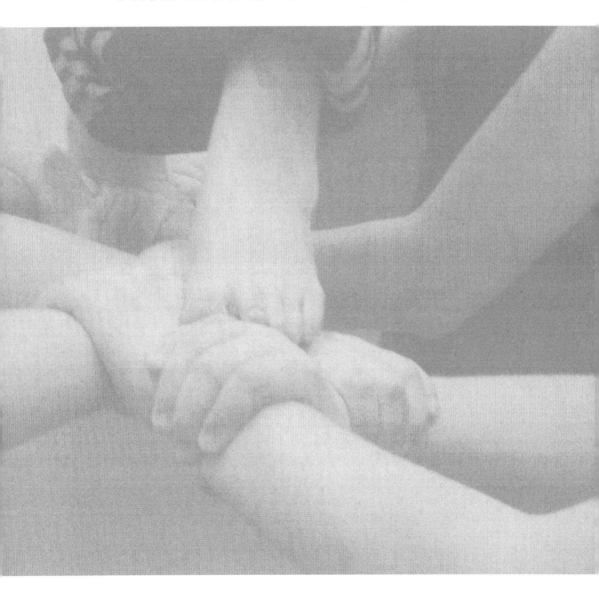

10

Dance in a shifting landscape

Veronica Jobbins, with Linda Rolfe,
Kerry Chappell and Anna Craft

Education only flourishes if it successfully adapts to the demands and needs of the time. (Qualification and Curriculum Authority, 2005:2)

Having worked in education since the 1970s, I have had first hand experience of the numerous shifts and changes that have shaped the curriculum and teaching practice in English schools. I first worked as a London secondary school dance teacher before the national curriculum was introduced. Later, I became involved in dance education nationally, as a member and Chair of the National Dance Teachers Association for 20 years, striving to ensure a curriculum place for dance. Working at Laban since 1996, I bring a dance conservatoire's perspective from training dance artists, as well as leading and developing an extensive programme of creative dance projects in London primary and secondary schools.

Involvement in Dance Partners for Creativity (DPC) gave me an opportunity to reflect on schools dance practice today in light of the changes I have witnessed. When I began teaching In the 1970s, dance was emerging as an independent curriculum subject. It has survived and even thrived within the plethora of government curriculum changes and initiatives. We now face more curriculum reviews and greater urgency to provide an education system for our children that keeps pace with 'accelerating economic and technological change' (Gove, 2011), while also recognising our humanity and inherent creativity. The time is right to re-assess how dance fits within the complexities of school curricula and to assert clearly what and how we want to actively contribute to young people's education, rather than just being reactive to circumstances.

The DPC premise is that a performative culture is stifling creativity within school dance education practice. Pressures from assessment agendas were sacrificing individual pupils' creativity in favour of formulaic choreography that would meet externally prescribed targets from examination boards and schools' assessment policies. This chapter's opening quote from the secondary school curriculum review suggests that adapting is a positive strategy which leads to effective educational outcomes. Yet the DPC research was revealing that adapting was constraining and distorting dance teaching instead of encouraging and facilitating creativity and creative dance practice.

This chapter describes how three of the DPC creative partnerships grew within, responded to and were challenged by the performativity agenda. It demonstrates that school dance education has always changed to survive. It questions whether dance truly flourishes if it simply adapts successfully to the demands of the time.

Performativity versus creativity

The National Advisory Committee on Creative and Cultural Education (1999) raised concerns that British education was being driven by a narrow focus on literacy and numeracy. In response the Labour government introduced educational policies and financially significant initiatives that encouraged creative and cultural learning in schools. The most notably were: Artsmark (2000, www.artsmark.org.uk/), Creative Partnerships (2002, www.creativepartner ships.com, a new Secondary Curriculum (2008, www.qcda.co.uk, and Find Your Talent (2008, www.findyourtalent.org/).

All in some measure promoted partnerships with arts and creative partners to support the curriculum and teaching and learning across all subjects, not just the arts. But there was a perceived tension between these policies and those promoting a very different agenda around what Ball calls performativity (outcomes-orientated teaching and learning):

> It is the data-base, the appraisal meeting, the annual review, report writing, the regular publication of results and promotion applications, inspections and peer reviews that are mechanics of performativity. (Ball, 2003:220)

Dance educators expressed their concern that performativity was negatively affecting school dance (Ackroyd, 2001; Chappell, 2008), reflecting similar issues in other subjects (eg Craft and Jeffrey, 2008). In response the DPC research sought to examine how creativity is conceived and facilitated and to question dance education practice. The interaction between external and school partners provided a catalyst for debate in which the proposition about performativity consistently emerged as relevant. Caroline, a school partner, commented:

> As teachers, we are governed by assessment frameworks and ... in our school we've just adopted a new lesson planning format ... to a certain extent, [it] lend[s] itself to what we do in dance, because it is about setting aims and objectives. It is about a creative task that they will explore. They'll connect with it, they'll explore it, they'll try it out, they'll learn from it, they'll adapt. They'll refine their ideas and come out with an outcome. But it is very much in that order. And sometimes it's nice just to be able to start with something and let it just drift in the manner that you want.

That collaboration with an external dance partner provided the impetus to move away from these constraints was acknowledged throughout the project. Caroline said: 'Right from the beginning we established that's not what this is going to be about, we're going to break the rules, we're not going to have the confinement of the curriculum'.

Entrenching the known or exploring the unknown?

Inherent within all art form education is a dynamic tension between teaching the art form skills and facilitating learners to be innovative and creative. Teaching dance skills in schools is generally related to choreography (eg understanding motif development or using canon), the physical technical skills of dancing and performing, and critical appreciation.

Emerging strongly from the DPC data was the recurring question: how much were choreographic structures or tools needed within a creative learning environment, as opposed to the importance of so-called freedom that encouraged students to create in an unrestrained way?

Were dance teachers influenced by performativity emphasising learning about tools at the expense of individual exploration? Were they more concerned to meet the demands of schools' agendas than they were about the subject itself? Was school dance teaching in danger of entrenching the known rather than exploring the unknown and determining what was valuable for teaching the art form itself?

DPC produced rich evidence that partnerships should encourage pupils' independent thinking as a pre-requisite for creativity. Accordingly, the East of England site (Chapter 5) placed equal emphasis on teaching for independence and teaching for creativity. Helen, the East of England school partner observed:

> One of the things that I have a really big issue with in schools is this idea that actually students aren't encouraged really to be independent learners any more. It's all about results and it's down to the teachers to make sure those students are getting results further on up the school.

Including students in discussions during the dance-making process was seen as vital to encouraging independence. It helped develop students' awareness and confidence in being creative, in the creative process itself, and especially with being confident about dealing with ambiguity. As one school partner pointed out, their creative project was not defined by an outcome at the beginning, as in the usual working methods, but was left open to evolve. Ambiguity allowed students to think independently and increased their motivation. In Helen's words:

> One of the things about the project that's so satisfying is that you haven't written on the board a learning objective and you haven't said by the end of the lesson you will all be able to do X, Y and Z ... the students aren't necessarily aware of it, and to see them, the interest and enthusiasm, because they just don't know.

The influence of performativity was also apparent in other teaching strategies. External and school partners used open ended questions to promote student learning and stimulate new ideas or ways of moving, but the school partner generally focused their questioning narrowly. The following London site quotation illustrates this:

> Bim (external partner): I think the way I encourage students to learn is through asking them open ended questions like how could you do that differently or what could make that more exciting ...

> Caroline (school partner): When I went round each group I would question them and ask them, well what are you doing, how can you improve that, how can you use your focus, how could you adapt the dynamics to make it more interesting.

The external partner encouraged students' responses that allowed autonomy in deciding the direction of creative tasks. The school partner used language which suggested a finite outcome to be judged against external criteria.

Dance assessment criteria of examination board syllabi will inevitably in-fluence teaching. Understandably, the school partners talked about building the students' knowledge base, with regard to the examinations, through Key Stage 3 to GCSE (General Certificate of Secondary Education). Whereas, the external partners wanted to stress dance's physicality as a mode of learning.

As Bim, the London site external partner, said: 'I would like them to have an internal experience of physical reality'.

The tension existed between how much the dance curriculum should include knowledge about dance choreographic tools, and how much about open-ended creative dance experiences. A balance between the two was favoured rather than one being taught at the expense of the other. Bim wanted to know:

> Are you trying to get them to explore, what are we trying to give them? Are we trying to give them tools to work with that can then adapt their movement material, or are we trying to get them to see how they can explore an idea? I don't know.

How much do pupils need a safe environment provided by clear teaching structures, before they can be confident to try something new and unknown? Or does excessive structure restrict students' imaginative and creative responses? The external and the school partners agreed that if students were to enjoy true artistic and creative practice, it was essential to allow them to be spontaneous, experiment and take risks beyond their experience and knowledge. As Helen said: 'There's no right or wrong to do it; it's allowing all to succeed.' But this approach was directly opposed to schools' performativity agendas, which constrained students by compelling them to meet prescribed teacher-set targets.

There was evidence that some whole school policies prescribed repetitive teaching frameworks or so-called structures to promote learning which were at odds with creativity. Caroline, the London site school partner, found that she was:

> ... very governed by lesson plan structure, what I have to cover, try, connect, explore, review ... and I have to have an element of talk because we're really focusing on the quality of speaking in our school, but if we're being creative, there's no time for that. It's about creating and using our bodies.

Process or product?

> The process is what creates 'becoming'; young students becoming artists, the school as a place of becoming and therefore I believe it is important to place particular emphasis on this part of the project as it certainly leads to the longevity of excellence in schools, as opposed to one excellent work. (Lîla Dance, South-East England external partners)

Unsurprisingly, there was much discussion in all the sites about process versus final artistic product. It could be assumed that schools which were influenced by the performativity agenda would be most concerned with highly polished dance performances that could be favourably assessed against clear external criteria. However, a more complex picture emerged. The schools did not dichotomise process and product but rather recognised their value and how they inter-related. Despite a tendency to polarise, they discussed whether or not experimentation was sufficient in itself; the value of a final dance performance; and acknowledged that the end product fed back to creative process and vice versa. Underpinning all the discussion was anxiety about spending time on the process at the expense of producing a polished project performance. Caroline pondered this balance:

> I think we both agreed actually, does creativity always have to come up with an end product. But I think, you know, we need to give something back to the students. I think the students need to know where they're at and I think they need to realise how they're moving on with it if you like and have a sense of purpose.

The East of England site project plan included an informal performance. Both school and external partners emphasised its positive outcomes. Michael, the external partner noted that:

> There is a degree of creativity in that they had to connect the physical and the imaginative aspect ... that extra leap of engagement ... that's a very creative act, not the creative building of the work but the performance with the intention.

The performance was seen as a special space to embody experience, develop commitment to the movement and ownership of the process.

Performing an end product was seen as also having value to the whole school community. It is a tangible demonstration of a creative project's worth and provided a shared experience. In the East of England site, Helen reported that: 'performances of the work created demonstrated awareness of creativity ... in engaging the audience and for them to understand that this is not just a creative process but a creative final outcome'.

Other external partners, however, expressed anxiety about the pressure to deliver a highly polished, professional performance on which they would be judged, when this conflicted with the original project aims. As one South-East external partner said: 'It's really hard as an artist not to think of the end product, so what I'd like to do is be brave enough to really value the process'.

Professionalism: becoming or being?
Within a school culture of high expectations as proposed by the current Secretary of State for Education, professionalism is highly valued: being

professional is about aspiring to achieve the best one can. Within arts education the external artists are generally seen to be bringing professionalism into the school. They are regarded as a positive role model, with special skills, knowledge and expertise, setting high expectations and challenging students in ways unusual in normal school settings. As Bim, an external partner, said: 'I think I make it very clear to who I'm working with that I want the absolute maximum potential from every single person in that room, including myself'.

DPC's external partners used their professional expertise to induct students into becoming professional themselves. They did so in various ways but it was especially by developing students self-discipline, good behaviour and strong technical dance and performance skills.

Figure 10.1 shows the external partner at the centre of attention during a final performance rehearsal. It is clear that he is admired, respected and listened

Figure 10.1: External partner inducting students into professionalism

to attentively by the students as they prepare for their performance. The site university researcher observed how the: 'group stay focused as they practise – others not dancing sit and watch – don't distract ... dancers keep working – students rehearsing like dancers' – linked to 'good behaviour' 'self-discipline'.

Professionalism extended, secondly, to the pupils becoming professionals, especially within performances. 'We treat them as young professionals as opposed to children, and I believe they respond to this with a sense of responsibility', said Abi, a South-East England external partner.

The ability to engender good behaviour through rigorous self-discipline is seen by schools as one of the values of having arts projects and as intrinsic to dance or arts practice. As a primary Head teacher observing the East of England performance said:

> You know, there was not a giggle, there was not a smirk. They just really undertook it as a completely professional exercise, right from our youngest ones which are maybe some of them still nine, right the way through the teen-agers and then up to the Suffolk-college age.

The students themselves bought into this agenda and appreciated the challenges set by the external partners' high expectations. This was particularly evident during final rehearsals for performance. The students needed to work hard and not be 'like kids', as Abi put it, in their attitudes to rehearsal and their willingness to work at the piece's detail and on their performance skills. A student reinforced this: 'I think it was like if we want it to be a professional piece or if we want it to be like a children's piece, and it kind of makes you think ... Because she [Abi] knows we want it to be a professional piece, but that makes you think we need to work harder'.

We watched pupils becoming a professional through an apprentice-like process, saw the ambition of both partners' and pupils' as professional, especially within performance. The pupils were encouraged to take ownership of their work and their sense of responsibility was rewarded.

Implications for policy and pedagogy

The research highlighted how dance teaching has been influenced by the schools performativity agenda. But the lens of performativity reflects back on issues that have been inherent in dance education in schools since the 1950s when it first gained a place on the curriculum.

The mid-way model of dance in education developed by Jacqueline Smith-Autard (2002) suggested a schools dance teaching model that balances so called 'professional' and 'educational' models (see Table 10.1 below). The professional emphasised end product, skills, techniques and performing, the educational process, creativity, imagination, individuality and open methods. Her 'midway' dance education model balances these aspects. It proposes that the 3-strands of dance – composition, performance and appreciation – are fundamental to the content of the dance curriculum and teaching methodology and leads to artistic, aesthetic and cultural education.

The mid-way model is evident in DPC dance teaching practice. It combines aspects of creativity with development of skill and choreographic understanding, using a range of teaching methods including problem solving and directed teaching. However, the terms 'professional' and 'educational' no longer have the same meaning in DPC as they did when the midway model was developed. The model was a response to prevailing dance education practice that sought to reconcile the Laban based modern educational dance (MED) introduced in the 1950s, which emphasised personal expression and spontaneous improvisation, with the professional dance practice from dance

EDUCATIONAL	MIDWAY	PROFESSIONAL
Process	Process + Product	Product
Creativity Imagination Individuality	Creativity Knowledge of Imagination + public artistic Individuality conventions	Knowledge of theatre dance repertoire
Feelings Subjectivity	Feelings + Skill Subjectivity + Objectivity	Skill acquired Objectivity
Principles	Principles + Techniques	Techniques
Open methods	Open and closed	Closed methods
Creating	THREE STRANDS Composition Performance Appreciation OF DANCES Leading to ARTISTIC EDUCATION AESTHETIC EDUCATION CULTURAL EDUCATION	Performing

Table 10.1: Features of the art of dance in education model (Smith-Autard, 2002:27)

training institutions and artistic practice drawing largely on Graham-based contemporary technique and choreography. Such polarisation was a result of the dislocation between MED and professional dance. Since the 1990s, it has become less evident as the school curriculum and the professional dance sector changed.

Dance training institutions, many of which now offer degrees, recognise the need to broaden their curriculum beyond dance technique and use varied teaching methods to nurture future dance artists. Linda Rolfe describes how current choreographers use improvisation around tasks and frequently a lengthy investigative process to develop a work with their dancers (see Chapter 8), whereas 1980s choreographers relied far less on their dancers' creative contributions.

No longer founded on child-centred teaching but increasingly driven by a target led agenda, the current school curriculum provides a context in which dance has taken on more of Smith-Autard's professional dance context. This change is apparent in the GCSE and A Level (Advanced Level) dance syllabi. Personal technical performance skills and professional choreography studies are strongly emphasised, including the replication and manipulation of movement phrases and vocabulary derived directly from existing dances. The educational elements of creativity, imagination and individuality have seemingly diminished although dance examinations continue to include students' choreographic work in the final assessments.

The DPC research ended at a turning point for the English education system and with it for dance education, as the coalition government reviews and reshapes the national curriculum. Dance in schools flourished in the creativity and cultural environment of the past ten years. Dance's longstanding position within physical education and the promotion of sport and physical activity likewise encouraged dance provision as a contribution to combating children's obesity and poor health. Though potentially conflicting, these agendas seemed compatible when there was an agreed rationale for dance in schools that combined the artistic with the physical (NDTA, 2004). But with the changes in schools and professional dance practice are the teaching methods for dance education still relevant?

Just as dance teachers in the 1970s needed to re-connect with professional dance to re-define what dance education should be in schools, DPC has re-iterated the value of bringing schools closer to professional artists and practitioners who can be critical friends to teachers. Together they can provide an enriched and more rewarding student experience while exploring the crucial question of what is best practice for dance in schools.

While DPC has produced a complex yet clear picture of how creativity can be used and developed within dance teaching, it has supported Smith-Autard's aspiration of the midway model that combines professional dance practice with creative and choreographic experience. However, DPC advocates the need to allow time for and encourage non-prescriptive creative dance experiences that prioritise process, foster risk-taking and independent thinking and promote individual creative responses which balance skills and knowledge-based approaches.

The perceived polarisation of schools' dance practice and that of professional dance artists has faded. The permeability between school and external partners no longer places them at two ends of a spectrum. Instead DPC has built a partnership practice model that sees the interaction of their skills and expertise to provide school students with a creative dance experience that reflects current artistic practice and also the best teaching and learning methodology. This also illustrates how teachers and artists can learn from each other and thus sustain and develop schools dance practice.

Dance teachers have always adapted their practice to fit external policies in schools and elsewhere. Frequently viewed as non-essential or at the edge of the curriculum, dance in schools has survived and flourished because of its chameleon-like ability to fit in with the latest initiative, be it health, creativity or performativity as identified by DPC.

The educational climate is likely to become less hospitable to creative and artistic subjects like dance, so it is imperative that dance practitioners within and outside schools evaluate their practice and identify how a dance curriculum and teaching methodologies can meet the needs of the system.

As I suggested, 'dance only flourishes if it successfully adapts to the demands and needs of the time'. How do we retain dance education's wealth of experience built up over time, while recognising the changes in schools and the professional dance world? In the end, dance will have no meaning in schools unless it is relevant to the pupils. DPC's extensive evidence demonstrates how collaboration between teachers and dance practitioners, in or out of schools, engages, motivates and inspires young people. Those working in dance education need to remain alert and responsive to change, but also critical and questioning so they give young people opportunities that are relevant to them, their needs and the cultural environment in which they are growing up.

11

Not just surviving but thriving

Kerry Chappell and Anna Craft with
Linda Rolfe and Veronica Jobbins

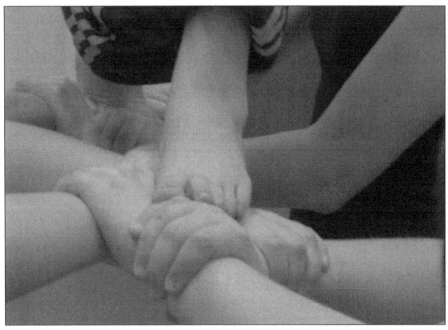

Figure 11.1: 'Close encounters'

This image captures a key moment in a collaboratively-devised piece of choreography in the East of England site, and represents the creative partnership characteristics and relationships in the Dance Partners for Creativity (DPC) initiatives. The 'close encounters' evidenced stimulated creativity in adults and students alike.

As discussed in Chapter 1, the DPC research aimed to capture these encounters, relating them to discussions about creativity, performativity, young people and partnership, and exploring how the various findings contribute to a case for different educational futures to those being perpetuated. The first part of this chapter synthesises the findings and their relationship to these discussions and the second part examines a specific part of the educational futures terrain and how DPC might contribute to it. What can the final set of principles from the research offer the practice of alternative educational futures?

Synthesising our findings

DPC had always been concerned that, despite creative partnership policies from 2000 onwards, creativity was being stifled by the constraints of performativity. By researching strong dance education creative partnership, DPC aimed to re-connect education practice with artform creativity. Research within DPC initiatives (Chapters 3 to 6) indicates that, amongst other approaches, original student choreography can be developed via:

- attention to partnerships, roles and relationships in relation to power and ownership
- application of imagery, ownership and feedback in collaborative choreography and creative engagement
- two kinds of partnership pedagogy – dance building blocks alongside wisdom of practice which intuitively ignites learning
- attention to the contribution of play to facilitating creativity framed through the lenses of time, space and relationship.

The findings of the partner researchers reveal the key ingredients for partnership practice to stimulate creativity. This goes beyond static, formulaic methods.

The DPC research also stepped back from these detailed close encounters to explore an over-arching question as detailed in chapter 2:

> What kinds of creative partnerships are manifested between dance-artists and teachers in co-developing the creativity of 11-14 year olds in dance in education, and how do these develop?

As we explored this we sought to answer three, often overlapping, sub-questions:

1. Roles and Relationships – What is the nature of partnerships? How were these co-constructed and experienced?

We documented genuinely flattened hierarchies in which students and adults crossed boundaries into new roles, fluid identities and leadership positions to build safe creative group environments. This represented a different kind of partnership practice to the polarised views documented in existing literature. The DPC evidence provides a case for a greater role for the value of uncertainty and engagement by all partners. Partners within and beyond schools developed specialist communities of practice, through mutual engagement, joint enterprise and via shared repertoires.

2. Conceptions of Creativity – What conceptions of creativity emerged through partnership? How was this manifest in enabling students?

DPC revealed how creativity was fundamentally humanising. The partnerships stretched students to develop new identities which generated new ideas which in turn fed these identities in a process of 'becoming'. The partners remained ethically mindful of the consequences, grounded in the reciprocal relationship between collaborative generation of new ideas and identities development. DPC revealed how dance education offered ethically-guided creativity which is rigorous, risky and empowering, an antidote to dominant agendas of marketised and individualised creativity, performativity and youth as needing to be protected from harm.

3. Problematising Creativity and Creative Partnerships – What tensions and dilemmas do partners face in enquiry-focused partnership?

DPC shed light on tensions in partnerships. It revealed how, when challenged by performativity, dance flourishes if it successfully adapts to those demands. But it also confirmed that unless dance is relevant to young people, it has no purpose or meaning in schools. DPC research-focused partnerships responded to tensions by 'meddling in the middle' – ie partners worked alongside students and actively engaged as critical enquirers alongside university researchers.

The big message?

This book has answered certain specific research questions. We have told stories from the different project layers located in practice, theory and policy and have aimed to provoke thought. One agenda has continually re-surfaced, however, across the DPC life-course: educational futures. Will education continue in the same vein as we know it? Would we like it to change? What will education in the future be for? What will it look like? Who will control it? What do we have to say and do about it?

On this final question, the university researchers have developed insights gained from involvement in the four DPC research initiatives, while also responding to the over-arching research question. This final section draws on our last layer of analysis and on our conversations with the partner researchers. Although their thinking is framed by a different theory-practice balance to ours, educational futures questions are as pertinent to them as they are to us. Our concerns and arguments have much in common with theirs, but we do not intend to speak for them.

We believe that the research can make a unique contribution by relating the work of DPC to current educational futures discourses. This chapter therefore takes a political direction, reaching into the policy framework for educational change. Below we examine the parts of the educational futures landscape which are pertinent to DPC, then discuss parallel debates within arts education and draw together the common concerns. We thus respond to key concerns in light of the final layer of DPC analysis.

The context of education now and educational futures

From DPC's perspective, creative partnership practice in education is currently dominated by the tensions described in Chapter 1. In summary, this means creativity that is characterised as individualised, marketised, globalised and harnessed to the performativity agenda which exists in tension with creativity that is characterised as wise, humanising, contextualised and challenging performativity. Partnership manifested through negotiation is in tension with polarised partnership. And this means tension between creative partnership where young people are seen as capable and empowered, and partnership where young people are seen as primarily at risk from harm and in need of adult protection. It was the growing imbalance towards performativity, marketisation, disempowerment and polarisation that initially triggered the DPC research described in this book.

Wide discourses of possibilities in educational futures have emerged simultaneously with DPC's research. Among the numerous educational futures areas, the one to which the DPC findings most strongly contribute is alternative educational futures and the distinction between probable, preferable and possible futures (Bussey *et al*, 2008). Probable futures are concerned with foresight: what is coming over the horizon. Preferable futures are those that we value and aim to bring into reality. Possible futures are the potential configurations we are open to. The DPC findings offer ideas for possible educational futures and open up further ideas for alternative futures.

Certain alternative educational futures analysts (eg Fielding and Moss, 2010) argue against the limited 'official' future offered by the policymakers, who articulate probable futures rather than diverse alternatives that acknowledge the fast pace of change outside education. We agree with their ethos of overthrowing the dictatorship of no alternatives. We also strongly agree with those attending to Education for the Future (Facer *et al*, 2011), whose authors argue that education needs to contribute better to sustainable futures.

Arts education: past, present and future

It is significant that arts theoreticians have highlighted arts education's unique role, even suggesting that it should be the basis for future education.

Abbs (2003) argues for the arts as a source of authentic education. He sees it as a necessity, providing the spirituality which consumer society desperately needs He, like DPC, acknowledges the debt to Reid's (1981) clarification of aesthetic education: the distinction and interrelation of 'knowing this' with other knowledge forms that is key to the unique contribution of the arts.

This is endorsed by Best (1992), who underscores the arts' contribution to the education of feeling. Ross (2011) goes further, arguing that the arts, with their inherent empathy and creativity, play a vital role in contemporary society's development. Robinson (2009) connects the arts with personal fulfilment. He argues that creativity and innovation are enhanced by attending to what inspires each individual in society to find 'the place where the things we love to do and the things we are good at come together' (pxiii). He calls this the Element and sees it as significantly nurtured by the arts.

Within this, dance makes its own unique contribution, as summed up by the English National Dance Teachers Association:

> As one of the major art forms, its [dance's] intrinsic value lies in the possibilities it offers for the development of pupils' creative, imaginative, physical, emotional and intellectual capacities. Because of its physical nature, dance provides a means of expression and communication distinct from other art forms (NDTA, 2004)

This statement affirms the assertions of Smith-Autard (2002) that dance contributes to developing sensory, expressive and formal qualities, a special combination of physically embedded feeling and form in aesthetic education. Bannon and Sanderson (2000) argued that if dance is to achieve its educational potential, greater significance should be given to this aesthetic element.

Smith-Autard argues that dance education makes a vital contribution to cultural education via its expression of heritage and identity through its myriad cultural dance forms. This resonates with Stinson's (2004) notion of the body as a source of knowledge, meaning and culture through dance. Citing Dewey, she argues that neglecting learning by doing wastes time and energy in schooling. Shapiro (1998) highlights dance's role in engaging the personal and the social, so allowing students to find their voice, and maintains that dance education is a uniquely transformative experience.

In the DPC findings we see these theoretical ideas demonstrated in practice. Melding together the push for alternative educational futures in the early 21st century with the weight of the ideas of arts education philosophers creates a framework for using the DPC findings to resolve some current concerns in education.

Common concerns

Current discourses about alternative educational futures and arts education philosophy have a number of pressing concerns in common:

There is a social, economic and environmental crisis regarding sustainability – more of the same is neither possible nor desirable; we cannot continue with an uncritical belief in the grand narratives of capitalist progress and growth. The concern over sustainability affects how we enact education.

The marketisation/globalisation of education is antithetical to a way of being which supports embodied individuals and their interaction within culturally-grounded community and which is necessary to re-frame our approach to education

The ongoing performatisation of teaching and learning, utilising externally (sometimes globally) imposed testing is increasingly dangerous. It constrains the communal, creative and humanising dimensions of education which might offer an effective response to these crises of sustainability and marketisation.

Centralised educational decision making which leans towards a protectionist view of both adult professionals and young people is stifling alternative educational futures. It is antithetical to roots-led change from empowered and capable practitioners and learners

How can we respond?
The purpose of education

These common concerns demand a re-evaluation of what education is for. This must be done before questioning what alternative or possible education might involve (Fielding and Moss, 2010). As poet Ben Okri (1999:65) said:

> The underground must be understood
> For the overground to be different

What does carrying out the DPC research tell us education is for? What is its 'underground'?

Fielding and Moss advocate what they call 'education in its broadest sense', a concept in which we find resonance, and define it as follows:

> ...fostering and supporting the well-being and development of children and young people and their ability to interact effectively with their environment and to live a good life ... education is a process of upbringing and increasing participation in the wider society, with the goal that both individual and society flourish. (p46)

Whole Education, a collection of organisations recently set up to gather aspirations for 'rounded' education (www.wholeeducation.org) argues that education is for all learners and broader than school, and that it must be adaptable and creative, and involve more than knowledge. It must be able to: nurture learning through life; ignite every individual's potential; and build resilience through relevant, active and engaging learning. Similarly The Coalition for Education in the 21st century (www.c4e21.org) has published principles foregrounding a well-rounded education for all, which is broad and balanced and develops skills, attitudes, knowledge and understanding alongside intellectual, practical, creative, aesthetic, physical, spiritual, moral, social and emotional capabilities (Mills *et al*, 2011).

Building on these ideas, we would argue that 21st century education has a responsibility to develop individuals who can make an ethically-grounded, humane and sustainable contribution to their societies and environments. Education is therefore about thoughtfully, diligently and creatively developing and empowering individuals so that they and their communities thrive socially and spiritually, and perhaps economically, but without a dominating emphasis on the latter. This can be achieved through paying attention to the emotional, physical, aesthetic, rigorous and critical, through attention to intrinsic as well as extrinsic values, through individual, collaborative and communal endeavour, and by working to navigate beyond 'what is'.

Thus we are offering an alternative aspiration to the dominant educational discourse. We need to remember that we do have choice over the broader performative educational framing. We need to collectively gain a better sense of possible new journeys beyond the current dominating frame. Fielding and Moss foreground the possibility of commonality between personally-held and societally-useful values. Inayatullah (2008) argues that such value alignment is vital in envisaging and enacting alternative educational futures. So our next step is to think about how we can align values in this way to provoke and enact alternative educational futures in light of the DPC project.

A quiet revolution

According to Fielding and Moss (2010) and to Eisner (2004), grand revolution is not the best way to establish common ground between personally-held and societally-useful values and to make change happen. More effective is to determine what education is for and then take a bottom up approach, an 'incremental, cumulative and reactive process' (Fielding and Moss, 2010:2). Eisner suggests that within the arts we need:

> ... to generate other visions of education, other values to guide its realisation, other assumptions on which a more generous conception of the practice of schooling can be built. That is, although I do not think revolution is an option, ideas that inspire new visions, values, and especially new practices are ... the arts can serve as a model for education (2004:4)

We are already in many cases making the change or could be making it in small but potent ways. DPC believes it can contribute to this quiet revolution by providing a methodology of creative learning conversations and Living Dialogic Space (see Chapter 2) which offer a way of conceiving of alternative educational futures. DPC can also offer understandings of dance/creativity/ partnership as possible (as opposed to preferred or probable) futures. Finally, especially through the final layer of analysis described below, DPC may provoke the active development of other educational futures.

Living principles of creative partnership practice

Grounded in our detailed findings, and to be applied with reference to them, the DPC university team conducted a final layer of analysis. This has generated a set of creative partnership principles to be used provocatively within the quiet revolution.

Three of these living principles (ownership, difference and dialogue, and quality) underpin all the others:

■ **Ownership** – This refers to who owns the creative process and related learning and how ownership is negotiated within partnerships; it relates to questions of power and is about nurturing students to take expressive ownership over their own roles, to embody ideas, and have their own voice. Complex distributed ownership is key to adults being able to flatten hierarchies as far as possible and share control through 'meddling in the middle' when working alongside young people. Young people's ownership of education more generally is crucial. Dance, other curricula and teaching methodologies need to focus on the needs of young people rather than the wider system, to make education relevant to them and increase their ownership of learning

■ **Difference and dialogue** – Partnership practice and research mechanisms have to engage in dialogues involving difference. Through cyclical learning conversations which value partial perspectives, the dialogues acknowledge and articulate tensions within partnerships and can trigger change. Partnerships can, for example, capitalise on the disruption of multiple identity and leadership position shifting. By raising the awareness of tensions, dialogues can contribute to stretching partners, launching them into riskier research territory, collective endeavour, more fluidly-defined roles and looser framing of teaching. Dialogues of difference can also raise and respond to tensions found in partnership policy and practice, for example between performativity and creativity, the known and the unknown, process and product, and different kinds of professionalism.

■ **Quality** – this perhaps most subtle principle emerging from DPC relates to value judgements of professionalism, expectations, originality and rigour. Judging value or success involves critiquing quality of creative process, wisdom of practice and student experience. This can be especially useful in attempts to redress the performativity and creativity imbalance, to find better ways to assess the quality of participants' journeys and their outcomes.

These three fundamental principles infuse each of the other four DPC principles: embodiment, professional wisdom, communal cohesion and generative possibility.

■ **Embodiment** – this is the connection between body and mind ie bodies and minds interacting together in creative partnerships for meaning making, understanding and communication. This connection can be modelled by adults, and is crucial to creative flow and to students fully engaging in movement. Embodiment underpins a humanising approach to creativity in which the creative process is embedded in young people as the substance of creative ideas; they are making and being made. Although this is an obvious principle to draw from dance, we suggest it is pertinent beyond; creativity can be practiced by connected bodies and minds in any discipline, embedding creativity within people

- **Professional wisdom** – that is, the wealth of teaching information and expertise that practitioners develop about their own practice, a deeply contextualised knowledge, often informed by intuition. In co-researching with experienced expert practitioners, DPC has encouraged professionalism which puts wisdom and intuition to the fore. This can jar with performativity agendas but doing so allows partnership practitioners to experiment, de-construct, self-direct and judge their successes, failures and next directions. It allows for critique and provocation beyond what is currently accepted; it is not about 'one model fits all'

- **Communal cohesion** – this is a connectedness that stems from the idea of shared group identities creating a kind of social glue. It is about allowing for difference more than uniformity, but there is a shared creative process and purpose. Such cohesion is often grounded in family-style relationships, which create a safe, mindful artistic space within which people can create together. Partnerships can provide enormous potential for involvement in this kind of shared space between worlds – in our case between dance and education – which have the capacity to create new ideas and influence change

- **Generative possibility** – this principle is strongly related to ownership and its underpinning power structures. This possibility has the potential for generativity, ie developing new ideas or even new spaces between all partners which then actualise creativity through other principles discussed here, such as ownership and communal cohesion. For example, when adults flatten hierarchies and 'meddle in the middle' to work alongside students, they open up 'possibility spaces' which in turn allow for creative journeys to take place over time. Generative possibility can be thought of, in terms of spaces created but also in terms of how time and relationships can be manipulated to catalyse different ways of teaching which can generate new ways of learning.

Navigating beyond performativity

Taken together, the three fundamental principles and four further principles enable a single common thread: the potential for creative engagement not to ignore or quash the performative demands of education but to re-frame and navigate beyond them.

As represented in Figure 11.2, through humanising, collective, democratic, multi-voiced activity, successful DPC partnerships were able to nurture ownership, difference and dialogue, and quality; and so nourish professional wisdom, communal cohesion, embodiment and generative possibility. Our analysis of the greater principles at play helps us to understand how creative partnerships were able to move beyond performativity and the formulaic choreography criticised in Chapter 1 and to nurture authentic adult and student creativity.

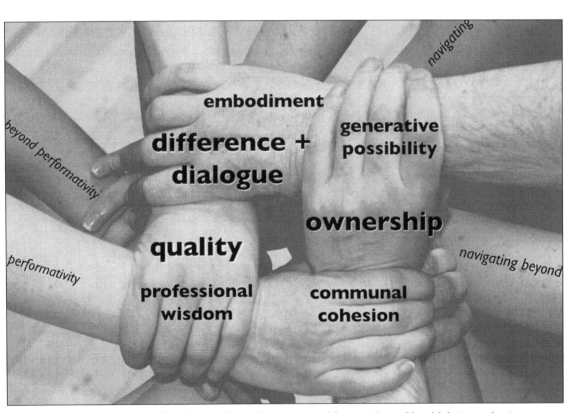

Figure 11.2: Principles of creative partnership practice with which to navigate beyond performativity

Provocations for change

We aim to use the DPC findings and emergent living principles to design pro-vocations for developing new practices and thinking. Returning to Bronfen-brenner's layered system (Chapter 2), we can see how we might strategically begin to initiate change within and hopefully between system layers.

We hope ultimately to influence change, particularly through the multi-faceted roles held by our large and varied professional team within the system. These roles are often combined and include those of researcher, prac-titioner, manager, teacher trainer, professional development leader, teacher, artist, and policy advisor.

In the final part of this chapter we present an example provocation for practi-tioners interested in research/enquiry, grounded in DPC findings and prin-ciples. This example can be a starting point for developing alternative edu-cational futures ideas and practices, no matter how small or large. By framing them within Bronfenbrenner's layered system we hope to indicate how changes can contribute in a cumulative way to the quiet revolution.

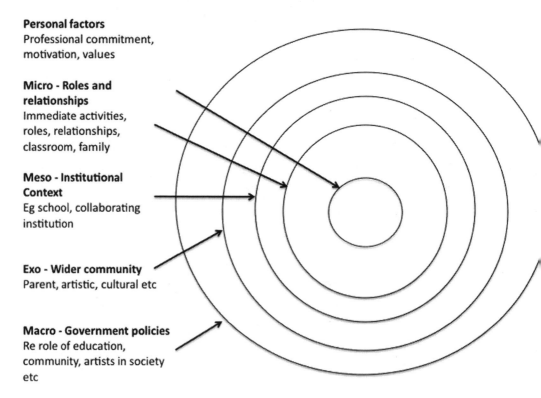

Personal factors
Professional commitment,
motivation, values

**Micro - Roles and
relationships**
Immediate activities,
roles, relationships,
classroom, family

**Meso - Institutional
Context**
Eg school, collaborating
institution

Exo - Wider community
Parent, artistic, cultural etc

Macro - Government policies
Re role of education,
community, artists in society
etc

Figure 11.3: Bronfenbrenner's layered system

Personal level

Personal level change centres on professional commitment, motivation and values. You might begin by finding small ways to chisel out time for professional development that excites you, triggering your curiosity and creativity. If so, ask

- How can partnership professional development be meaningful for you and an achievable part of practice over which you have some control?

- How can this development include *your* ongoing learning about your discipline and its practice beyond the curriculum that's relevant to you?

- How can it include *your* thoughts on what education and creativity are for?

- How might being playful help make debate and uncertainty a more everyday part of teaching and learning?

- How, over time, can you question what is taken for granted in your working systems, and take bigger steps to make changes?

Roles and relationships level

This level foregrounds immediate activities within roles and relationships. It might involve unpacking relationships with students and colleagues, questioning taken-for-granted roles and informally and formally seeking out new roles and relationships.

- Who/what controls your roles and relationships and what changes might you be able to make and why?

- Who might your 'partners' be and why: (eg students, colleagues outside your discipline)?

- What is the partnership's purpose and how is it relevant to the adults and young people involved?

- How can you set up partnerships, which include students, which afford time and space for negotiation and quality review?

- What for you and your partners is creativity? Is it different for each of you? What does that mean within your partnership practice?

- How might you get involved in informal or formal communities of practice that keep your curiosity and creativity alive and support you in your changes?

Institutional level

This level broadens out from immediate relationships into the wider organisational context in which you work, be that a school, an arts organisation or company, a charity or a university. The change you can make obviously depends on your position and leverage within the institution. (If you are not institutionally-based, making changes will require different thinking.)

- Can you creatively re-assess how you allocate resources (time, space, relationships, people's expertise, funding) to support your partnership's educational ideas and activities?

- Where constraint from performativity is slight, eg in out-of-hours school groups, non-touring company time, how can space and time be used to experiment, play and risk-take? How can outcomes be appropriately applied back into the institution?

- How can you together open up manageable longer term institutional spaces for reflective, creative conversations between partners (colleagues, students and parents) which support debate and ensure positive practical change?

- How might these spaces embody and encourage your partnerships' values, ethics and collective aspirations over time; and perhaps build communities of practice?

- How might these reflective spaces, communities and ensuing activities ultimately contribute to shifting institutional structures, power relationships and policies?

The wider community level

Taking into account the myriad media within which we can all be part of communities, this level is at the same time the most dispersed and yet possibly the most potent for achieving educational change. Wider community exists formally and informally in the innumerable physical and geographical communities around you and your institutions, as well as the face-to-face and virtual communities centred around your educational ideas, activities and discipline. Working within this level moves questioning beyond the immediate and stretches ideas and activities for change out into society. Opening up conversations between institutional/organisational contexts and wider communities and emphasising two-way influence may be the starting point.

- What mechanisms and media can you make use of in order to create flexible boundaries between your institution and the communities around it: people, digital media, culture, arts, business, research?

■ What outside possibilities are there to bring in resources from communities around you to support your educational endeavours: people, time, funding, expertise?

■ What quality criteria, approaches to professional development and learning exist in other disciplines and in your surrounding communities that might be debated and adapted to support your educational ideas and activities?

■ How can you make stronger relevant connections between the communities that are important and exciting to both young people and adults, particularly within schools, to fuel your partnerships' educational ideas and activities?

Policy level

Unless we are professionally connected to policy-making, this level can seem the most far-removed part of the system, whether or not we have voted for those making the policies. However, through accumulation within and across the layers above, and through digital means, it grows easier to exert influence at this level quietly but meaningfully.

■ How can you take advantage of flexible spaces within policy as they arise while working with others eg the present UK government's spotlight on professional autonomy? How can your partnerships translate such spaces into meaningful support for educational ideas and activities?

■ How can you develop collective communal responses when there are few supportive policy spaces? Via, for example the current UK campaign for a richer Baccalaureate (http://abetterbaccalaureate.org/), or by contributing to the recent national curriculum review through bodies such as the NDTA (www.ndta.org.uk)

■ How could your work be informed by how you view your own agency (as directed by yourself or others) and your foresight (how certain do you think you can be about what the future holds?) (see Facer *et al*, 2011)

■ How might you bring together local ideas with global debates within communities or disciplines to give them more weight eg via World Alliance for Arts Education online debates?

These provocations can be applied cumulatively through the systemic model and are aimed at enquiring practitioners. Other provocations might be developed from the DPC principles for students, teacher trainers, educational managers etc. In this way different people can be triggered to contribute to the quiet revolution towards alternative educational futures.

Navigating tensions

The DPC project was intentionally located between the creativity and peformativity narratives, and the DPC principles described in this book illustrated how creative engagement can navigate beyond performativity. We close with a return to this navigational theme. Inevitably tensions are inherent in all educational aims. On the one hand the neo-liberal narrative argues for education as servicing the needs of a globalised economy. It is concerned with accountability, systems where individuals' actions are judged in relation to the whole institution's performance. This accentuating of performativity is intertwined with the social crisis of sustainability in education, the dominance of marketisation and the disempowerment of adults and young people alike. On the other hand, and in contrast, is a narrative of education as being of creative worth. This narrative emphasises creativity, self- and social fulfilment, and well-being. It prioritises the personal over the societal.

Yet whilst societal performativity and personal creativity are frequently polarised – and this was where our study began – the research has revealed vividly that these conflicting aims are inseparable in practice. Teachers and artists in DPC experienced the pressures and opportunities of both sets of aims, the discord between performativity and creativity. But DPC has shed light on how these conflicting narratives may be navigated via wise, humanising creativity which broadens the notion of what education is for and how it relates to society.

We have made the case in this book that education needs to be imbued with greater creativity, communality, humanity, empowerment and negotiation and that an uncritical belief in growth and progress is mistaken. We synthesised a set of principles from across the research which can be applied to support individuals interacting in partnership within culturally-grounded communities. They suggest an alternative to driving people on to striving competitively within marketised performativity frameworks. By providing this applied example of the principles translated into a multi-layered practitioners' provocation, we have demonstrated how meaningful change can be triggered from the bottom up.

Where next?

In early 2011, as the DPC project closes, we are encountering opportunities for multi-level engagement in which small-scale advocacy connects with big picture educational change. The government announced a review of the English National Curriculum in January 2011 that would detach the notion of 'entitlement' and the aims and purposes of education from provision. The consultation, on four proposed 'core knowledge' areas (maths, science, English and Physical Education) occurred alongside the introduction – without warning – of the English Baccalaureate, which excludes the arts.

At a time when the arts appear to be very low on the British government's agenda, action is needed. The DPC findings and principles may bring the potential of intensive arts-education initiatives to the attention of policy-makers. We hope that DPC's living principles and their accompanying provocations will be able to throw a lifeline to individuals and initiatives which would otherwise tread water in wait for the next wave of supportive policy. If they apply the DPC ideas, they might continue to thrive rather than merely survive. As poet Ben Okri so eloquently puts it, 'we need to become adaptive mariners' (1999:48). We need to support each other from our complementary positions within the larger system.

There is still much to do. We need to keep revisiting what education is for, keep looking within our discipline expertise – in this case dance – to see what we can offer each other to help make the changes needed, and to keep incrementally, cumulatively, proactively fuelling the quiet revolution. Ben Okri's words of wisdom end this book:

> Our future is greater than our past ...
>
> ... Tradition doesn't have to weigh us down.
>
> We weigh ourselves down with tradition, ...
>
> ... We have made these things
>
> We can unmake them ...
>
> ... We should begin to think anew.
>
> To prepare ourselves for a new air,
>
> For a fuller future ...
>
> ... For we are each ...
>
> ... co-makers of the world we live in ...
>
> (*Anti-spell for the 21st century*, 1999:53-54)

References

Abbs, P (2003) *Against the flow: Education, the arts and post modern culture.* London: Routledge Falmer

Ackroyd, S (2001) *But is it creative?* London: Seminar, Arts Council of England, July 2001

Bakhtin, M M (1984) *Problems of Dostoevsky's Poetics.* Ed and trans. by Caryl Emerson. Minneapolis: University of Michigan Press

Ball, S J (2003) The teacher's soul and the terrors of performativity. *Journal of Education Policy* 18(2) pp215-28 Mar-April

Banaji, S, Burn, A and Buckingham, D (2010) *The rhetorics of creativity: a literature review. 2nd edition.* London: Creativity, Culture and Education

Bannerman, C (2004) The artist and the process of creation. *ESRC Seminar*, 5 July 2004, Christchurch University College, England.

Bannerman, C, Sofaer, J and Watt, J (2006) *Navigating The Unknown: The creative process in contemporary performing arts*, Middlesex University Press

Bannon, F and Sanderson, P (2000) Experience every moment: aesthetically significant dance education. *Research in Dance Education*, 1(1), pp9-26

Bennett, N, Wood, E and Rogers, S (1997) *Teaching Through Play.* Buckingham: Open University Press

Best, D (1992) *The Rationality of Feeling*, London: Falmer Press

Bragg, S, Manchester, H, Faulkner, D (2009) *Youth Voice in the Work of Creative Partnerships.* Milton Keynes: The Open University

Briginshaw, V (2001) *Dance, space and subjectivity.* Basingstoke and New York: Palgrave http://opencreativity.open.ac.uk/recent.htm#previous_papers (October, 2010)

British Educational Research (2004) *Revised Ethical Guidelines for Educational Research.* Nottingham: BERA. http://www.bera.ac.uk/files/guidelines/ethica1.pdf (January, 2011)

Bronfenbrenner, U (1979) *The ecology of human development.* Cambridge, MA: Harvard University Press

Bruce, T (1991) *Time to Play in Early Childhood Education.* Sevenoaks: Edward Arnold, Hodder and Stoughton

Burnard, P and Swann M (2010) Pupil perceptions of learning with artists. *Thinking Skills and Creativity.* 5 (2) pp70-82

Bussey, M, Inayatullah, S and Milojevic, I (eds) (2008) *Alternative educational futures: pedagogies for emergent worlds.* Rotterdam/Taipei: Sense Publishers

CapeUK (2009) *On TAPP: professional development for artists and teachers.* Leeds: CapeUK

Castle, K, Ashworth, M and Lord, P (2002) *Aims in Motion: dance companies and their education programmes.* National Foundation for Educational Research

Chappell, K (2006) Creativity as individual, collaborative and communal. In *Proceedings of dance and the Child international conference*, The Hague, July 2006 (p42-53)

Chappell, K (2008) Towards Humanising Creativity. *UNESCO Observatory E-Journal Special Issue on Creativity, policy and practice discourses: productive tensions in the new millennium* Volume 1, Issue 3, December 2008 http://www.abp.unimelb.edu.au/unesco/ejournal/vol-one-issue-three.html (April, 2011)

Chappell, K and Craft, A (in press) Creative learning conversations: producing living dialogic spaces. *Educational Research.*

Craft, A (2005) *Creativity in schools: tensions and dilemmas,* Abingdon: Routledge

Craft, A (2008a) Trusteeship, wisdom and the creative future of education? *UNESCO Observatory E-Journal,* Volume 1, Issue 3, December 2008 *Special Issue: Creativity, policy and practice discourses: productive tensions in the new millennium*

Craft, A (2008b) *Voyages of Discovery: Looking at Models of Engagement.* Arts Council England Creative Partnerships

Craft, A (2010) 'Teaching for Possibility Thinking'. *Learning Matters,* 15(1), pp19-23

Craft, A (2011) *Creativity and Education Futures.* Stoke on Trent: Trentham Books

Craft, A, Gardner, H, Claxton, G, *et al* (2008) *Creativity, Wisdom and Trusteeship, exploring the role of education.* Thousand Oaks: Corwin Press

Craft, A, and Jeffrey, B (2001) 'The Universalization of Creativity', in Craft, A, Jeffrey, B, Leibling, M, *Creativity in Education,* London: Continuum (pp1-13)

Craft, A and Jeffrey, B (2008) Creativity and performativity in teaching and learning: tensions, dilemmas, constraints, accommodations and synthesis. *British Educational Research Journal* Vol. 34, No. 5, October 2008, p577–584

Department for Culture Media and Sport (2006) *Government response to Paul Roberts' review on nurturing creativity in young people.* London: Department for Culture Media and Sport

Department for Education (2010) *The Importance of Teaching.* London: The Stationery Office

Department for Education (2010) *Addendum (The English Baccalaureate).* At http://www.education.gov.uk/performancetables/Statement-of-Intent-2010-Addendum.pdf (21.01.11)

de Sousa Santos, B (1999) Oppositional postmodernism. In *Critical development theory,* eds R Munck and D O'Hearn. London: Zed Books

Dewey, J (Jo Ann Boydston ed) (1989) *John Dewey: The later work: 1925-1953. Volume 16.* Carbondale: Southern Illinois University Press

Eisner, E (2004) What can education learn from the arts about the practice of education? *International Journal of Education and the Arts,* 5(4): 1-13

Ellsworth, E (1989) Why doesn't this feel empowering? *Harvard Educational Review* 59(3): 297-324

Facer, K, Craft, A, Jewitt, C, Mauger, S, Sandford, R and Sharples, M (2011) *Building Agency in the Face of Uncertainty: a thinking tool for educators and education leaders.* ESRC Seminar Series

Fielding, M and Moss, P (2010) *Radical education and the common school: a democratic alternative.* London: Routledge

Freud, S (1908) Creative Writers and Day-Dreaming. In Dickson, A (1985) Arts and Literature: Jensen's Gradiva, Leonardo Da Vinci and Other Works. *The Penguin Freud Library Volume 14,* 129-141

Fuller, A (2007) Critiquing theories of learning and communities of practice. In Hughes, J, Jewson, N and Unwin, L (eds) *Communities of Practice: Critical Perspectives.* Routledge, Oxon.p17-29

Galton, M (2008) *Creative Practitioners in Schools and Classrooms. Final Report of the project: The Pedagogy of Creative Practitioners in Schools.* Cambridge: University of Cambridge

Gavin, H (2008) *Understanding research methods and statistics in psychology.* London: Sage

Gough, M (1999) *Knowing dance: A guide for creative teaching.* London: Dance Books

Gove, M (2011) *Commentary on the announcement of the National Curriculum Review in England.* Cited on Department of Education website, January 2011 www.education.gov.uk (April, 2011)

Griffiths, M and Woolf, F (2004) *Report on Creative Partnerships Nottingham Action Research.* Nottingham: Nottingham Trent University

Institute of Education (2011) *Concern that English Baccalaureate overlooks Arts subjects.* 18 Jan 2011. http://www.ioe.ac.uk/newsEvents/48992.html (April, 2011)

James, S and M (2000) Leaving school at 13. In Dowty, T. *Free Range Education: How Home Education Works,* p155-161. Gloucestershire: Hawthorn Press

Jeffery, G (ed) (2005) *The Creative College: Building a successful learning culture in the arts.* Stoke on Trent: Trentham Books

Jeffery, G and Ledgard, A (2009) *Teacher Artist Partnership Programme 02, Perspectives from the literature,* CapeUK

Jobbins, V (1999) Curriculum development: moving through the review process, *Dance Matters,* 24, pp2-3

John-Steiner, V (2000) *Creative Collaboration.* New York: Oxford University Press

Jónsdóttir, S R and Macdonald, A (2007, November) *The ecology of innovation education.* SERA Annual Conference 2007, Perth, Scotland

Lavender, L (1996) *Dancers talking dance: Critical evaluation in the choreography class.* Champaign, IL: Human Kinetics

LeCompte, M and J Preissle (1993) *Ethnography and qualitative design in educational research.* 2nd ed London: Academic Press

Lefebvre, H (1991) *The Production of Space.* Wiley-Blackwell

Leinhardt, G (1990) Capturing craft knowledge in teaching. *Educational Researcher.* 19 (2) 18-25

Lincoln, Y S, and Guba, E G (1985) *Naturalistic inquiry.* Beverley Hills, CA: Sage

McCarthy, T (1991) *Ideals and illusions.* Cambridge, MA: The MIT Press

McWilliam, E (2008) Unlearning how to teach. *Innovations in Education and Teaching International,* 45 (3) pp263-269

Merleau-Ponty, M (1962) *The phenomenology of perception.* Transl. C Smith. London: Rourledge and Kegan Paul

Merleau-Ponty, M (1964) *Signs.* Transl. R McCleary. Evanston: Northwestern University Press

Mills, G and the Coalition (2011) *Summary of Principles. Coalition for Education in the 21st Century.* www.c4e21.org (April, 2011)

Moje, E B, and Luke, A (2009) Literacy and identity: Examining the metaphors in history and contemporary research. *Reading Research Quarterly,* 44 (4), p415-437

Moran, S and John-Steiner, V (2004) How collaboration in creative work impacts identity and motivation. In *Collaborative creativity: contemporary perspectives,* (ed) D. Miell and K. Littleton, pp11-25

Munby, H, Russell, T and Martin, A K (2001) Teachers' knowledge and how it develops. In V. Richardson (ed), *Handbook of Research on Teaching (4th ed).* Washington, DC: American Educational Research Association, p877-904

National Advisory Committee on Creative and Cultural Education (1999) *All our futures: Creative and culture and education.* London: DFEE

National Dance Teachers Association (2004) Maximising opportunity. *Policy Paper* 2004. Burntwood: NDTA

Ofsted (2006) *Creative Partnerships: Initiative and impact.* London: Ofsted

Okri, B (1999) *Anti-spell for the 21st century: Mental fight.* London: Phoenix House

Prentice, R (1994) Experiential learning in play and art. In Moyles, J *The Excellence of Play,* p125-135. Maidenhead: Open University Press

Pringle, E (2008) Artists' perspectives on art practice and pedagogy. In Sefton-Green, J (ed). *Creative Learning. London: Creative Partnerships* www.creative-partnerships.com

Qualifications and Curriculum Authority (2005) *Futures – meeting the challenge.* London: Qualification and Curriculum Authority

Reid, L A (1981) Knowledge, knowing and becoming educated. *Journal of curriculum studies,* 13, 2

Robinson, K with Aronica, L (2009) *The Element: How finding your passion changes everything.* London: Allen Lane

Rolfe, L and Harlow, M (1997) *Let's Look at Dance.* London: David Fulton

Rolfe, L, Platt, M, Jobbins, V with Craft, A, Chappell, K and Wright, H (2009) Co-participative Research in Dance-Education Partnership: Nurturing Critical Pedagogy and Social Constructivism. *Conference on Research in Dance, Conference Proceedings* (p98-109). University of Illinois Press

Ross, M (2011) *Cultivating the Arts in Education and Therapy.* Abingdon: Routledge

Shagoury-Hubbard, R (1996) *A Workshop of the Possible.* Portland: Stenhouse Publishers

Shapiro, S B (1998) (ed) *Dance, power and difference: critical and feminist perspectives on dance education.* Champaign: Human Kinetics

Shusterman, R (2008) *Body Consciousness: A philosophy of mindfulness and somaesthetics.* New York: Cambridge University Press

Smith-Autard, J (2002) *The art of dance in education (2nd ed).* London: A & C Black

Sparkes, A (2009) Novel ethnographic representations and dilemmas of judgement. *Ethnography and Education.* 4(3) 301-319

Stinson, S W (2004) My body/myself: Lessons from dance education, in L Bresler (ed), *Knowing Bodies, Moving Minds: Towards embodied teaching and learning.* London: Kluwer Academic

Thomson, P, Jones, K and Hall, C (2009) *Final Report: Creative School Change Project. Creative Partnerships.* London http://www.creativitycultureeducation.org/research-impact/thematic-research/ (September, 2010)

Tishman, S and Palmer, P (2006) *Artful thinking: Stronger thinking and learning through the power of art.* Harvard University, Cambridge, MA: Project Zero

Vygotsky, L (1978) Interaction between Learning and Development. In *Mind and Society,* Cambridge, MA: Harvard University Press

Wegerif, R (2010) *Mind expanding: Teaching for thinking and creativity in primary education.* Maidenhead: Open University Press

Wenger, E (1998) *Communities of Practice; learning, meaning and identity.* Cambridge: Cambridge University Press

Index

WHAT PEOPLE SAY ABOUT *CLOSE ENCOUNTERS*

As a tertiary educator, arts education policy writer, classroom teacher and parent, I recommend this book to you. Read it. Imagine a curriculum that genuinely invigorates your children's education. Visit your local school and begin the dialogue using this research to foster an understanding of how education can be better.

Close Encounters examines practice and theory that shifts and shapes creative partnerships between teachers, artists and students. As the title of the book infers, teaching/learning partnerships that value creativity may inspire better educational encounters. Together with the practitioner researchers involved in the research, the highly experienced authors ask parents, teachers, artists and future educators to consider the implications when we place creative empowerment at the axis of education: what would education in the future look like if it gave dance-based creative partnerships the space to foster children's creativity? This book begins to answer this question, with thorough research that critically offers insights into teaching strategies, the role of professional artists' intuition, importance of play and collaboration, and challenges emerging. **Associate Professor Ralph Buck, Head of Dance Studies, The University of Auckland, New Zealand**

Close Encounters raises key questions about the importance of creativity in the curriculum as a whole and provides plenty of evidence for the beneficial impact of fostering the creative approach, particularly with its emphasis on risk-taking and empowerment. At a time when the arts may appear to be under threat in the curriculum because of government policy ... this project provides a useful reminder of the value of finding time for creative learning conversations. The book offers a valuable example of the ways in which universities, schools and practitioners can work together to investigate areas of interest to all. It can be difficult for schools to make time for this kind of work but the importance of taking time to reflect on what we are doing and why cannot be underestimated and this project shows how powerful the outcomes of that can be. **Claire Robins, Headteacher, Sir John Lawes School, England**

A refreshing approach to the challenges of creative partnerships, the book steps beyond some of the superficial perceptions of partnership, to share deep insights into the nature of effective long term, reflective partnerships.

Rooted in both practice and research, the book blends the authentic voice of practitioners, artists, researchers, children and others in a rich mix. It digs deep into their experiences and reflections to explore some of the complexities and challenges of partnership work, offering insights which will be of value to anyone interested in partnerships between artists and teachers in school. The book models 'living dialogic space' which the authors argue are at the heart of creative partnerships. They skilfully weave together different perspectives and creative learning conversations, making the concepts accessible and tangible, and they conclude with an inspiring call to take a leap into imagining a future for education with creativity at its heart. **Pat Cochrane, CEO, CapeUK**

At a time of predetermined learning outcomes and performance targets, the research described in this book reminds us of the need to refocus on the importance of creative engagement in the art of dance. Whilst creative partnerships between artists and teachers are rare in schools, the book's exposure to the 'living principles' that emerged from artist/teacher reflections and theorists' analyses will definitely inspire teachers to develop creativity by being adventurous, opening doors, re-defining their roles as teacher-artists and taking up the challenges presented in the final chapter. The book provides a much needed call and rationale for change in dance education and education generally. **Dr Jacqueline Smith-Autard, Author and co-director of Bedford Interactive (multimedia resources for dance)**

It's brilliant to read research that walks its talk – or dances its steps. This non-hierarchical collective of researchers, dance artists, and teachers tells vivid stories of inquiry that reveal false starts and missteps, satisfactions, and the puzzling recognitions of and reflections about these along the way. This work is creativity from beginning to end; the research is creative, as is the teaching, as is the student learning; together, the text informs the broad reach of educator-readers. Bravo for such a rich, coherent, and transparent portrait of the timely and vexed topic of creativity. **Lois Hetland, Professor of Art Education, Massachusetts College of Art and Design Senior Research Affiliate, Project Zero, Harvard Graduate School of Education.**